PUCKER FACTOR

STORIES OF MACVSOG

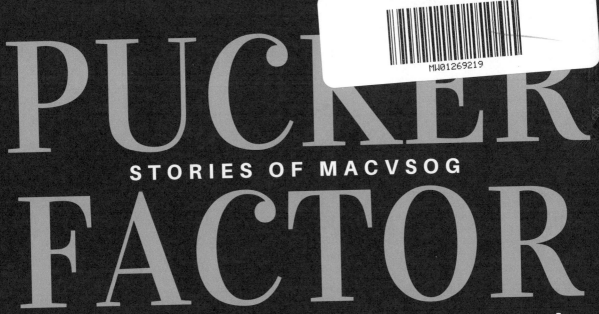

From the Veterans in their own words

VOLUME 1 ISSUE 3

By Jason B. Collins

Table of contents

Editors note: As you read these stories please take a moment to remember those that did not make it home and some that are still unaccounted for.

"A man is only truly dead when he is forgotten"

SGT JOHN T WALTON

By John Stryker Meyer

In the early days of our friendship, we exchanged family notes: my dad was a milkman, his dad "had a five-and-dime store" in Bentonville, Ark., and we had strong, no-nonsense moms. In May 1968, we were young Green Berets who had just entered the secret war that was fought during the Vietnam War. We were stationed at FOB 1 in Phu Bai as members of small reconnaissance teams that ran top-secret missions across the fence into Laos, Cambodia, and North Vietnam.

In August of '68, on one such mission, Walton's six-man recon team was surrounded and overrun by enemy soldiers. The attack was so fierce, that the team leader called an airstrike on his team to break the enemy attack. That strike killed one team member, wounded the team leader, and severed the right leg of the Green Beret radio operator Tom Cunningham Jr., of Durham, N.H. Another team member was wounded four times by AK-47 gunfire by an enemy soldier whom Walton killed.

A South Vietnamese helicopter pilot, Capt. Thinh Dinh, landed and picked up the five living members of the team while under heavy gunfire and barely extracted the team from its sure-death firefight with hundreds of enemy soldiers.

On 3 August 1968 a reconstituted RT Idaho, led by One-Zero Wilbur Boggs, inserted into the Ashau Valley about ten miles from where the old RT Idaho had vanished on 20 May. Boggs' One-One, Specialist Four John Walton, was an accomplished poker player, friendly, intelligent, and a talented medic capable of surgery. Idaho's One-Two was a new man, Private First Class Tom Cunningham.

Not long after insertion, swarms of NVA descended on RT Idaho, and soon One-Zero Boggs was seriously wounded, two 'Yards' were dead and the team immobile, hopelessly encircled by NVA so close Walton could see smoke from their cigarettes. With the team about to be overrun, young Walton did the only he could and called an air strike practically on top of RT Idaho, which hit friend and foe alike.

The NVA pulled back. It took every bit of Walton's medical skill to keep his wounded teammates alive, though Tom Cunninham would lose a leg. That anybody made it out is attributable to Walton's courage, cool head and medical ability. He was awarded the Sliver Star.

SGT'S MEYER - BOGG'S - WALTON

John Thomas Walton was born in Newport, Arkansas, the second of three sons, and excelled at athletics. He was a standout football star on their public high school football team and was more of a student of life than academics. His father, Sam, opened Walton's 5&10 in Bentonville, a small business in a small town known for its variety of hunting seasons. Walton had a modest upbringing and after only two years of college he dropped out to enlist in the U.S. Army. "When I was at Wooster [The College of Wooster in Ohio], there were a lot of people talking about the war in the dorm rooms, but I didn't think they understood it," Walton said.

Walton enlisted in the Army and became a Green Beret (Army Special Forces). "I figured if you're going to do something, you should do it the best you can," he said during an interview with Andy Serwer for Fortune magazine. Assigned to MACV-SOG after the Tet Offensive in 1968, Walton was stationed at FOB 1 in Phu Bai where members of Strike Team Louisiana conducted deep penetration reconnaissance missions. John Stryker Meyer, a teammate and friend of Walton's, wrote, "In August of '68, on one such mission, Walton's six-man recon team was surrounded and overrun by enemy soldiers." The firefight became so intense that the team leader, William "Pete" Boggs, called an airstrike (napalm) directly on their own position to break contact.

"That strike killed one team member, wounded the team leader, and severed the right leg of the Green Beret radio operator Tom Cunningham Jr., of Durham, N.H. Another team member was wounded four times by AK-47 gunfire by an enemy soldier whom Walton killed," Meyer wrote. As the team's medic, Walton was responsible for setting up a triage point to tend to the casualties. He applied a tourniquet to Cunningham's leg which had begun to hemorrhage. The tourniquet ultimately saved his life, but he later lost his leg. Facing hundreds of North Vietnamese soldiers (NVA) and surrounded, Walton called in two extraction helicopters.

The first helicopter, piloted by South Vietnamese Captain Thinh Dinh, touched down and picked up members of the team, some of whom Walton personally carried. The enemy soldiers were now sprinting to prevent their escape. Bullets clanged off the chopper and whizzed by their bodies. A second helicopter was needed to get them all out, but realizing how dire the situation had turned, the first helicopter sat back down and picked up the entire team. Their weight was too much, and they barely managed to climb over the treetops. Walton's determination to get his teammates out of harm's way earned him the Silver Star, the nation's third highest award for valor.

During a poker game on the night they returned to base, one of his teammates noticed that the skin on Walton's wrist was burnt. It was evidence of just how accurate the NVA gunfire was. Walton, Meyer, and his teammates enjoyed poker, Scrabble, and other games that require thought. They spoke about their goals and the dreams they hoped to accomplish when they returned home. Walton's was a life of adventure.

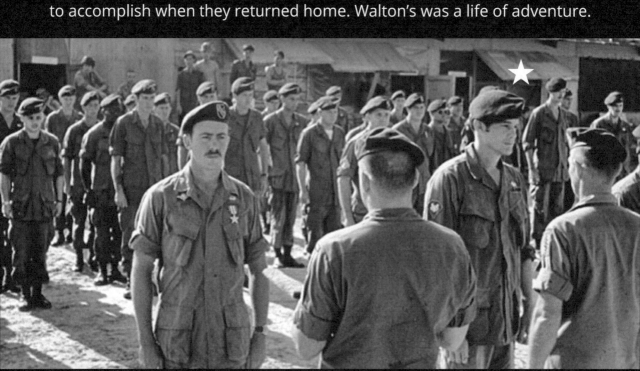

Walton on right receiving Silver Star

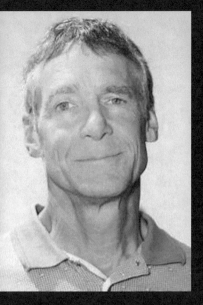

Sadly on June 27, 2005, his CGS Hawk Arrow home-built ultralight aircraft that he was piloting crashed in Jackson, Wyoming. He was only 58 when he lost his life doing something he loved, flying.

A personal Side of John Walton
By: J. STRYKER MEYER – Staff Writer

The headlines announcing the tragic death of John Walton focused on the personal fortune he had amassed as the second of three sons of American icon and entrepreneurial pioneer Sam Walton, the founder of Wal-Mart.

Since 1968, the John Walton I knew was first and foremost a family man —- when his father was dying of cancer, he flew around the world searching for remedies to the disease that ultimately claimed Sam Walton's life.
He was an intelligent free spirit who went his way in life —- becoming a Green Beret medic and succeeding in the businesses he started while extolling the virtues of charter schools.
Yet, the man who died on June 27, 2005, when his ultra-light aircraft crashed in Grand Teton National Park, was the same, humble, caring man I first met 37 years ago in Phu Bai, South Vietnam.

J. STRYKER MEYER

DEADLY RESCUE

30TH OF JUNE 1970

By Retired LTC Mike Taylor

**Capt. William S. Sanders
AKA "Bungalow Bill"**

MACV-SOG operated a super-secret launch site (Heavy Hook)

at Nakhon Phanom, Thailand, largely because there were two monsoon seasons and often when Vietnam weather was unworkable we could launch, support, and extract teams. The launch site was assigned to CCN for admin and logistics but under the operational control of MACV-SOG OP-35 (Ground Studies Group). In addition to two CH-53 helicopters and four A-1 Skyraider escorts, our daily air asset package included three sorties of OV-10 or O-2 Forward Air Controllers from 23rd Tactical Air Support Squadron "Nails". The first bird would launch early in the morning with the launch site's dedicated FAC Rider aboard and they would regenerate for the third sortie. The second sortie would cover their absence with a different FAC pilot with a back seater from the launch site for whom "Riding Covey" was an additional duty.

North American Rockwell OV-10 Bronco
Similar to the one flown by Capt William Sanders

On June 30th, 1970, pilot Captain William S. "Bungalow Bill" Sanders, "Nail 44", and SFC Albert E. Mosiello, "Heavy Hook' FAC rider, was conducting a visual reconnaissance mission in an OV-10 #3807. Due to mission requirements for close-up handheld photography, Nail 44 was flying at an extremely low altitude under 1500ft which was the minimum for aircraft in the AO. The aircraft was taken under fire and hit by a 37mm AAA shell on its left side immediately adjacent to the pilot's position. With his pilot unresponsive and the OV-10 no longer airworthy, Al Moseillo was forced to eject. Al's back was injured in the ejection and he only had a pistol with which to defend himself. The OV-10 went down in heavily forested, rugged mountains about three miles west of the Lao/South Vietnamese border and twelve miles south of the demilitarized zone (DMZ). Our second FAC in the vicinity, planning to relieve Nail 44 on the station, with CPT Mike Taylor, NKP Ops Officer, in the back seat, heard Al Mosiello's emergency beeper and made contact with Al. We located Al and initiated Search and Rescue operations. A CH-53 Jolly Green Giant rescue helicopter from the 40th Air Rescue/ Recovery Squadron (ARRS) at "Udorn Royal AFB, Thailand" was immediately dispatched.

SFC Albert E. Mosiello

The CH-53 (aircraft #8283) CALL SIGN "Jolly Green." The crew consisted of :

Pilot Capt. Leroy C. Schaneberg

Co-Pilot Maj. John W. Goeglein

SSgt Michael F.Dean Pararescueman

Ssgt Paul Jenkins

MSgt Marvin E.Bell

As the aircraft hovered over SFC Mosiello's position it was hit by an RPG in the rotor head. The rotor assembly separated from the fuselage, which rolled over and crashed in a stupendous fireball on the ground. It seemed no one could have survived. No emergency beepers were heard from the helicopter's crash site and we could see no sign of survivors. Although nightfall was approaching, a second effort was staged using a second Jolly Green Giant helicopter from Da Nang and A-1 " Sandy's" for fire suppression. SFC Mosiello

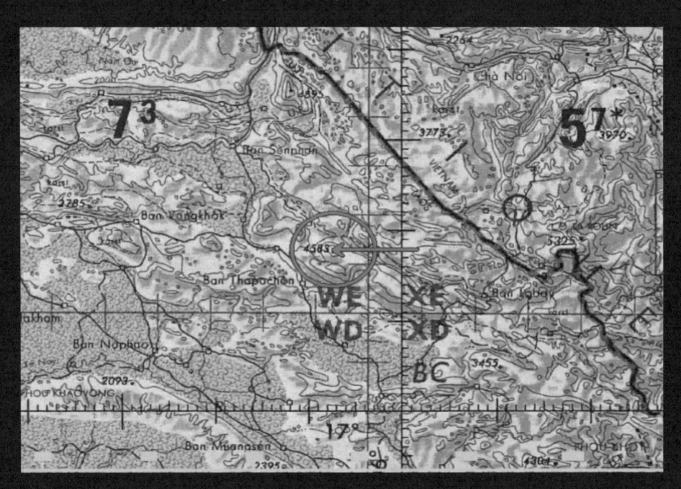

Location of crash site 165004N 1063104E (XD617617)

was successfully extracted. In his debriefing statement, SFC Mosiello stated his belief that Capt Sanders had been killed by the direct AAA hit and that he did not see Sanders eject or another parachute deploy. Search efforts for Captain Sanders and the first HH-53 crew continued through the next day, but no beepers were heard, no contact with the downed aircrew was made, and there were no visual sightings of survivors either. SAR efforts were terminated and the six men were listed as KIA / Body not recovered.

I cannot describe the pucker factor involved while watching the heroic crew of the second Jolly Green approach Al, low and slow, directly over the site of the loss of an entire crew and a helicopter identical to theirs only a short time before. They were flying over their comrades' fiery graves in an effort to rescue one of my best friends, a man they had never met. Thank God, they succeeded.

In December of 1992, a U.S / Lao recovery team surveyed and excavated the CH-53c crash site. Human remains were recovered and on 7 March 1995, the U.S government identified the remains as those of the five HH-53 c air crewmen. Efforts to locate the OV-10 crash site were unsuccessful due to the terrain and dense jungle.

Bill Sanders was an outstanding pilot and a suburb Prairie Fire Forward Air Controller who did an outstanding job supporting the men of SOG on the ground. He died way too young and his body has yet to be recovered. I shall always remember him as such a good man, a good pilot, a great FAC, and a better friend.

God bless you, Bill Sanders,
From a friend and comrade-in-arms

Nail 44. *Mike Taylor*

**FACs riders from left Jim Latham, Mike Taylor, Dick Hall,
Pat McCaslin, Butch Musick, Garry Robb and Dan Gibson**

Additional information

The second helicopter crew that rescued Mosiello consisted of Major James Z. Elkinton pilot, Capt. Dale R.Clark co-pilot, SSgt John C. Alcorn flight engineer, and SSgt Jules C.Smith pararescueman.

Before Mosiello was winched up to safety and assisted by pararescueman Smith, A1s dropped tear gas on the surrounding area to incapacitate the approaching NVA forces.

Recovery of the crash site in 1992 of Capt Schaneburg's crew yielded 120 bone fragments, a dental prosthesis, and a partial I.D tag. The I.D tag belonged to Michael Dean and the dental prosthesis to Paul Jenkins.

At the time of this publication, no remains of Capt Sanders's pilot of the OV-10 have ever been found. He is still one of the many unaccounted-for servicemen who served in the Vietnam war. You are not forgotten, Sir,

Martha Raye

By J.B. Collins

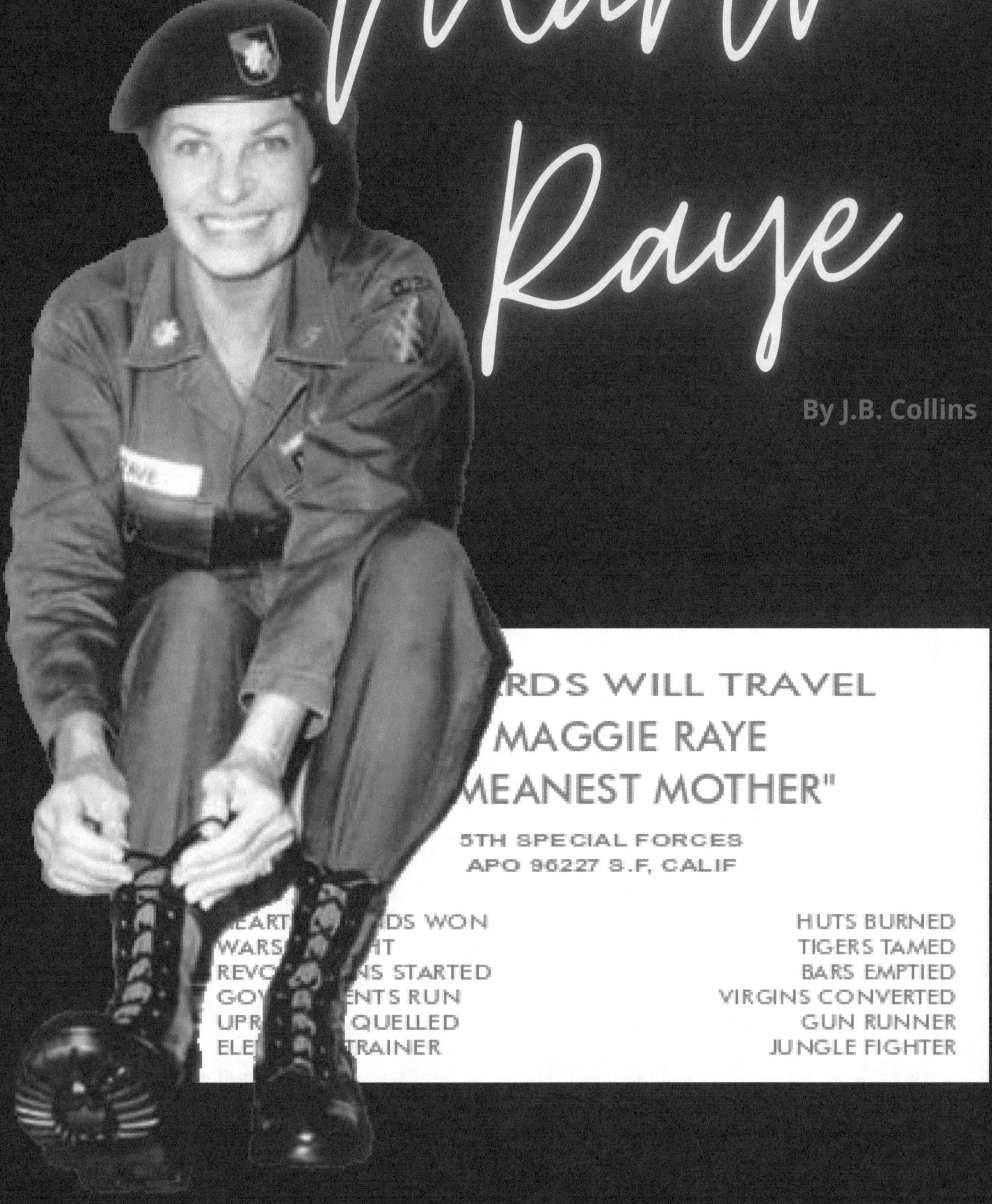

RDS WILL TRAVEL
MAGGIE RAYE
MEANEST MOTHER"

5TH SPECIAL FORCES
APO 96227 S.F, CALIF

HEART   NDS WON
WARS   HT
REVO   NS STARTED
GOV   ENTS RUN
UPR   QUELLED
ELE   TRAINER

HUTS BURNED
TIGERS TAMED
BARS EMPTIED
VIRGINS CONVERTED
GUN RUNNER
JUNGLE FIGHTER

Born Margy O'Reed on August 27, 1916, in Butte Montana to parents Peter F O'Reed Jr. (an Irish immigrant) and Maybelle Hazel from Montana, both amateur actors.

She quickly found a passion for the stage first appearing in her parent's act called "Reed and Hooper" at age 3. Her rise to stardom began to get underway in her early thirties as a singer. It wouldn't be long before the world would see her on the silver screen starring in movies with Hollywood's elite of the day including Bob Hope, W.C Fields, Jimmy Durante, and many more.

The World as she knew it was about to change in a multitude of ways that would forever be etched in history at the start of America's involvement in WW2.

USO Tour ETO WW2   Algeria February of 1943

   Being a patriot Marta Raye joined the USO in 1942. This began a love affair with the soldiers of the United States armed forces. Throughout WW2 Raye would travel with the USO to far-off locations around the world making soldiers, sailors and airman's lives a little better if only for a short period. An extreme fear of flying did not stop her from entertaining the troops during WWII, the Korean War, and the Vietnam War.

*But Martha's true love was those men who wore the **Green Beret** during the Vietnam war.*

MY FRIEND

By LTC David Carr

Maggie

My association with Martha (Maggie Raye) was long and never dull!!

We first met on 19th October 1967 in DaNang where I was assigned at the time to A 107 Tra Bong A site in I Corps. I had flown from the A site on October 19 to bring papers and assorted ash and trash stuff to the C Team in DaNang. On the morning of the 10th of October, I was told to report to the CO'S office (LTC Dan Schungl) and he pinned my 1st LT's bar on me and I got to remove the dreaded 2nd Lt bar! He told me to be in the club in the evening and I could buy him a drink. Maggie had flown in late in the afternoon and was present in the club when I walked in. She had just arrived and threw a $50 bill on the bar and said that buys for now (remember drinks were like 20 cents a piece so that equates to a lot of drinks!)

Met her again at CCN in DaNang. She flew in and partied with the guys till the early morning hours. I was picked to wake her up at 09:00 hours to catch a helo......I banged on her door multiple times.... no response. So I gently opened the door and said "Maggie your chopper leaves in 15 minutes...) place was like a bomb went off, fatigues and underwear strewn all over the floor....she lifts her head and calls me ..##@###! but finally gets out of bed and is ready to go and gets to the chopper on time!

Next time we see each other is Ft Ord in 1971. I was stationed there in the Training Command 3 shop....and a few of us Special Forces vets said lets invite her up to party. She accepted and we had put out the word to the whole Post and reserved the NCO club to host her. ABOUT A 125 FOLKS CAME OVER TO SEE HER..I MC'd the event which included MG Hal Moore, CG of Ft Ord. It was a great time and everyone got to enjoy Maggie and her performance. Gen Moore and I met at the Airport and returned her to the Airport in Monterey in his staff car. While waiting for her to depart ,MG Moore asked me about my experiences in Vietnam, never once telling me of his valorous battles there. A very great man!

The last time I saw her was 1982. She came into St. Louis for the performance of "Four Girls Four" with Helen O'Connell, Kay Star and Rosemary Clooney. A bunch of us SF guys went to see her it and I presented flowers to all four in their dressing rooms before the show, I got big kisses from all four! After the show concluded Maggie wanted to see us in her dressing room. A few of us went back there and saw her. She invited us all to stay and party and drink with her and all four stars which we did till late in the night. While I was backstage waiting to take Maggie to the after party there were a number of people at the back door for the stars to come out and get autographs. Well Maggie was not quite in the mood for some reason. A few folks pleaded with me please please get her to sign their programs...so I went back inside too see Maggie was not in the right mood right then. Not to disappoint her fans I signed the best Maggie "I love you signature " I could, and handed them to the wide eyed admirers, who thanked me very much. Oh boy ..what you will do for a famous star!

She was one in a million and we miss her very much!!

David Carr

Sitting in my family room in St Louis........watching the movie "Patton" on TV with Martha (Maggie) Raye.........she was telling us all about her USO tours in North Africa and England.............meeting Patton, Eisenhower and Omar Bradley, among others.......!

St Louis 1980 would be the next time Maggie and I would meet. I was stationed at the Army Records Center and a bunch of SF vets asked and were granted an opportunity to establish an SF Chapter in her name...Martha RAYE SFA Chapter. We flew her in for an inaugural party...she and her admin assisant stayed at my house for three nights. Talk about a wild and wolley 3 days..HOLY COW! Never knew they bottled that much Vodka. MG Iron Mike Healy flew in also and we had a big shindig at the local VFW Hall with many folks in attendance. She wowed us all and we were thrilled to host her. After returning to L.A, Maggie got in the habit of calling me about about midnight her time 2AM my time...She was feeling no pain from the nights before unlike me. She loved Col Splash Kelly, CSM Bowser and many other names I have since forgotten. We would talk for about half and hour. It happened so often that as soon as the phone rang at 2AM my wife would nudge me and say...."*There's Maggie for you*"

From left CPT David Carr, SGM Marvin Compton, Martha, CPT Steve Wyce, unknown

1969

Maggie visits

The photo with Martha Raye and myself took place in December '69. We were both on the same Chopper. While waiting for another ride, I got the picture. She chewed out a major for not saluting her. Anyway, a few days later at CCN, someone noted that she had been taken over to Charlie Company, which is next door to CCN. So a friend and I took a jeep over and found her at the O-Club. We told her she was at the wrong SF location and brought her back to CCN. She spent a little time with us in our small O-Club and then went over to the EM club. She stayed much of the night there...sang songs and drank vodka straight. Next day she left from our helo pad and I never saw her again. She was quite a lady. But I know a lot of other guys on the SOG board have some great stories about Maggie.

Capt Michael Miller

Commander, Company A CCN.

LTC Jack Warren, CO, CCN.

LTC Jack Warren gifted Maggie the 1-0 jacket you see here in these photos.

Maggie and Charles 'Wes' Wesley at CCN.
This was one of his most prized photos.

THE TALES OF MARTHA'S PARTYING ARE ENDLESS..

HAVE YARDS WILL TRAVEL
LTC MAGGIE RAYE
"THE MEANEST MOTHER"

5TH SPECIAL FORCES
APO 96227 S.F. CALIF

HEARTS & MINDS WON
WARS FOUGHT
REVOLUTIONS STARTED
GOVERNMENTS RUN
UPRISINGS QUELLED
ELEPHANT TRAINER

HUTS BURNED
TIGERS TAMED
BARS EMPTIED
VIRGINS CONVERTED
GUN RUNNER
JUNGLE FIGHTER

This is the card that Martha Raye gave me when she came to visit her guys at CCN in 1969. We had a small room set up as a bar where we all donated our chits to keep the bar supplied. For some reason, I seem to recall that she was drinking vodka tonics. She was just like being one of the guys although she loved hearing me tell her how much my family back home loved watching her on T V. Unfortunately I was only able to spend about an hour with everyone because I had to get back to the TOC .

SP4 William R Ressegue

Maggie was given this SF ring as a thank you for everything she had done for the boys. AP wirephoto 1966

Martha asked for a

"SALTY DOG"

The salty dog cocktail is a three ingredient drink that is composed of grapefruit juice, vodka (or gin) and sea salt.

Martha sat on the bar between Smitty and I who were on bar stools and introduced herself and then asked the bartender for a "Salty Dog". She wore a green beret and her camouflaged fatigues had jump wings, both American and Vietnamese, her rank that of a full colonel. Also on her fatigues she had caduceus which designated her as a nurse or doctor. Her Salty Dog arrived and I asked what it was. She explained it was Vodka and grapefruit juice with a salty rim and would I like to try one? She asked me if I would like to hear some songs, absolutely ! I said. She belted out " I left my heart in San Francisco". I felt compelled to give her something back so I gave her my Buddha medallion. It was a great night, one I never forgot

Excerpt from a story by *K. Rasemen 67-71*

Jack Webb, Martha and Ken Bird, CCN

Jesse Campbell

RT IDAHO / RT INDIGO
T41AE

I met Maggie coming off an C-130 at CCN 1969. We had just returned from a mission.

She had all kinds of brass with her. **I told her if she wanted to party with some real men** to come see me. Don't know how she found us but she did come and party. The lady drank straight gin. She is seen in the middle photo tasting rice wine. It was a wild night.

SOG and Naval officers hang out with Maggie

Maggie meets SCU Recon Team member in CCN club

Maggie entertains crowd

Cletis Sinyard (Babysan) on right. Larry Trimble next to Maggie with a mustache. Also Randy Givens and SGM Nameth closet to camera is Jim Lamotte.

I took that photo in the summer of '71 just outside the entrance to the NCO Club at the CCS compound. It hung in every locker I used after my DEROS until I retired, then I put it under the glass on my desk at SF Command when I started my 2nd career as a loyal civil servant. Like all young SF guys in the late 60s & early 70s I heard stories about Maggie, she was a legend. When she came to visit us at CCS/TF3AE I knew I'd get my chance to meet her. Oh, did I meet her ...
Maggie and the old guys sat on the elevated floor in the club, she drank Vodka over ice (I think) out of a water glass. One of my senior NCO buddies (I was an SGT) asked me if I'd been up to meet her. I said no. He told me that Maggie just finished making a movie with Jane Fonda, and when I got my turn I should ask her how she liked working with Fonda .. of course, I did. I met Maggie, told her where I was from, that it was my first tour, and that I'd heard stories about her since I arrived at Bragg. Then I basically asked her, "One of the guys said you just finished making a movie with Jane Fonda, and I was wondering how you liked working with her ..." Wrong thing to do. The air immediately turned blue with Maggie saying something like "Jane Fonda!? #@## Jane Fonda! That communist bitch ..." and on and on. Of course, everyone knew I'd been set up, so everyone got a good laugh at my expense. Maggie hugged me.. and that was that.
As we continued to drink I wondered if Maggie had seen the gun truck we had to provide security for the guys running to Nha Trang for supplies. Without asking I went to the motor pool, fired it up, and drove it to the club, parking it over the sidewalk that led to the entrance. I walked in and announced that Maggie should come outside and see what we had for her. She did. I had my camera so I snapped that photo. She loved it!

In the early 70s, my CCS vet buddy Tom Cook (RIP) carried the picture with him when he went to California to spend a couple of days at Maggie's safe house. I asked him to get Maggie's autograph which he did.

I was diagnosed with cancer in '05, and not knowing if I was going to live or check out I took the picture out to the National SFA HQs and gave it to one of the officers for safekeeping. Obviously, I beat cancer, but I never saw the photo again. Bad decision on my part .. I've always regretted making it.

There's more to the story involving an author who wrote a book about Maggie. In the early 90s, I loaned the photo (the original) to the SF Command Illustrator who was helping him gather info for the book. He used my photo as a chapter lead in (Chapter 5, I believe) and claimed credit for it. I tried to contact him to set the record straight, but my efforts were unsuccessful.

Chris Crane

Martha Raye died on OCT 19 1994

Special Forces Honor Martha Raye At Bragg

FORT BRAGG, N.C. (AP) — Army Special Forces soldiers honored Martha Raye on Saturday at a funeral that began with Green Berets bearing her flag-draped coffin to her grave and ended with her jazzy theme, "Mr. Paganini."

Her raucous rendition of the song in her 1936 debut movie, "Rhythm On The Range," with Bing Crosby, made her a star. Through three wars, she worked tirelessly to entertain U.S. troops.

Raye, who died Wednesday in Los Angeles at age 78, had requested a grave at Fort Bragg, home of the Green Berets who knew her as "Col. Maggie."

Normally only active and retired Army personnel are buried at a base, but the Special Forces Association asked military brass to make an exception, and they did.

An honor guard from the 7th Special Forces Group Airborne served as pall bearers. The 82nd Airborne Division band played patriotic songs. And about 300 soldiers and civilians came to honor her.

Raye appeared in numerous mov-

ies and TV shows, and had her own TV series, "The Martha Raye Show," in the 1950s. In later years, she was best known for her denture adhesive ads.

Raye received a special Academy Award in 1969 and the Presidential Medal of Freedom last November for her support of the Army.

Retired Master Sgt. Tom Squire met Raye when she traveled into the Mekong jungle to entertain his unit of just 25 men during the Vietnam War.

"She came, regardless of the danger. She talked, drank, told jokes, played cards," he said at the funeral. "A lot of times, when the regular Army didn't know what was going on or understand, she would just go."

Raye often gave her home phone number and address to soldiers, and when they called, she greeted them like old friends, Squire said.

When Squire was wounded, Raye visited him in the hospital, he said.

"There were times I don't think some of us would have made it if she hadn't been there to brighten things up," he said.

The name Buddha means "one who is awakened" or "the enlightened one."

THE BUDDHA

By Dick Gamble

The photo below shows me returning to Phu Bai after a particularly bad mission. On the right you will see a big guy, I don't remember him being S.F I think he was assigned to handle supply or something like that. Well, he showed up wearing an "ivory" Buddha, about the size of a half dollar, around his neck. One day he was standing by the supply and was about 30 feet from him when I heard the rocket and yelled "incoming". He had no idea what was happening. The thing hit about 40 feet from him and he went down like a sack of rocks. I ran over to him as he was sitting up rubbing his chest. The Buddha was cracked and broken in half but had saved his life. The next week we were all sporting Buddhas!

Lt. Bauso & his "A" Company Hatchet Force third platoon
Special Commando unit @ FOB 4

August 23 1968
the worst Day in Special Forces history

The "**U.S military brass**" thought it highly unlikely that an attack would occur at FOB-4 at any time. It would turn out to be a costly mistake. With a year of detailed planning, an enemy force of NVA / VC sappers numbering an estimated 100 or more overran the base on a moonless night. These well trained Commando (Sapper's) had written on their bandana's **"chúng tôi đến đây để chết"** translated means " we came here to die".Most would be killed during the three-hour attack. It came as a complete surprise in the darkness of the late hours to the men of SOG and their indigenous counterparts. When the battle was over 16 SOG soldiers and 40 indigenous Soldiers would be lost.

*Those killed at FOB 4/CCN were; Ssgt. Talmadge H. Alphin Jr. *Pfc. William H. Bric III *Sgt. 1st Class Tadeusz M. Kepczyk *Sgt. 1st Class Donald R. Kerns *Sgt James T. Kickliter *Master Sgt. Charles R. Norris *Sgt Maj. Richard E. Pegram Jr. *1st Lt. Paul D. Potter *Master Sgt Rolf E. Rickmers *Spec. 4 Anthonly J. Santana * Master Sgt. Gilvert A. Secor * Sgt. James W. Smith *Sgt. Robert J. Uyessaka *Ssgt. Howard S. Varni * Sgt. 1st Class Harold R. Voorheis * Sgt. 1st Class Albert M. Walter * Sgt. 1st Class Donald W. Welch.*

A short time later it would be up to soldiers like 1st LT Phil Bauso / 1st 1LT Rodney D Burns/ Sgt Ray Johnson to Train a Nung quick reaction force to be ready for any mission sent their way.

1st LT Phil Bauso leading Third platoon out of FOB 4

1st LT Phil Bauso at the range firing a Swedish K

M-79

"Thumper","Thump-Gun", "Bloop Tube","Big Ed", "Elephant Gun," and "Blooper"

As it was called by the troops. It gave the soldiers the option of firing 40mm rounds of anti personnel, smoke ,buckshot , and flechettes rounds at an effective range of 350m - 383yds. Bauso is seen with a customized M-79 which was very common for SOG soldiers especially the men of Recon Teams when firepower was limited to what they could carry. The men of SOG often cut there's down as shown in the top photo.

Quick reaction drills

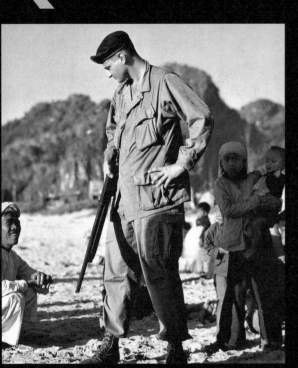

1St Lt Rodney Burns

Nung soldiers from third platoon.

Burns is seen here with a Chi-com K-50 enemy weapon. It was a high bred from the Russian WW2 PPSH-41, the PPS 43, and some elements of the French MAT-49. It became a well used weapon by the communist forces ,durable, dependable and capable of 35 rounds of 7.62 x 25mm in one mag. Popular until the availability of the AK-47 became more wide spread in war.

Marble mountain shootout

This report was written by LT Dan Thompson after speaking with eyewitnesses like Ken Bird, **Phil Bauso**, and "Smitty". LT Thompson and his platoon were ordered up the mountain to find Lenchner and find the hole in the top of the mountain and get the men out. Marble Mountain Shootout—14 December 1968, Quang Nam Providence, Republic of Viet Nam. During the preceding week, Major Moore, S-2, CCN, received actionable intelligence from a wounded POW. The same sapper unit that had attacked FOB#4 on 23 August had slipped back into Marble Mountain. Major Jack Deckard, S-3, sent "A" Company Hatchet Force (Nung) and two Reconnaissance Teams, RT "No Name" (PRU), led by Specialist John "Smitty" Smith and another RT (unk), to find, close with, kill, or otherwise drive the enemy from the mountain. Straphangers, LNO Captain Randy Givens (in the country for three weeks) LNO LT Francis Bret, and others are attached.

The first platoon, LT Dan Thompson, cordoned the western base of the mountain near old French Fort. One SCU was KIA and two WIA from the shoebox mine. In the second platoon, LT Fredrick Barbour drove deep into a large grotto. **In the third platoon, LT Phillip Bauso** stood in reserve. Upon entry into the dark, craggy confines, the 2nd Platoon came under withering crossfire that scattered the Special Commando Unit, SCU. Salvos of grenades and automatic fire wounded several SCU, Barbour, and two straphangers. The platoon was pinned behind rocks as dead and wounded lay exposed to enemy fire. Several attempts to reach the injured were driven back by intense automatic fire. The firefight raged throughout the morning. Each time reinforcements attempted to relieve the 2nd platoon, concentrated automatic fire drove them back. LT Barbour, straphangers, and six wounded SCU were driven deeper into the cave. Outside, the 3rd platoon engaged in a running gun battle with snipers positioned in caves and spider holes along the southeast wall.

TA CH-34 hovered in front of a cave midway up the southern slope of the mountain and exchanged automatic fire. The Kingbee, driven off, trailed smoke from its engine. The nine men, two with serious head wounds, were driven deeper into the cave. Short on ammunition and medical supplies, there was no way out except through a hole in the roof. They faced the imminent prospect of being overrun or hypoxia, from blood loss. Outside, Specialist Smith was critically wounded in a firefight and medevaced. Assessing the critical situation, LT Lenchner, without directive, climbed the mountain with rope and pistol. As 3rd platoon watched from below, weapons trained to provide cover, Lenchner secured rope, Swiss Seat and carabiner, and without fear or hesitation pushed off. The enemy sprung from the cave, fired and retreated. Lenchner fell mortally wounded.

LT COL Jack Warren arrived at the base of the mountain and asked for volunteers to retrieve Lenchner's body down. SSGT Ken Bird, RTO, observed men firing M-79 rounds into the cave. **LT Bauso**, friend and roommate, and the unknown officer responded. Using Lenchner's rope, Bauso rappelled down the mountain as grenades were thrown into the mouth of the cave. Bauso lowered the body down. For his actions, **LT Phillip Bauso** was awarded ARCOM/V. Late afternoon, the 1st platoon found a hole on top of the mountain. One each UH1-D, without a winch, failed to extract the trapped men and was driven off. By EENT 1st platoon had pulled LT Francis out by hand. That night, LT Barbour and straphanger were extracted by CH-53 as an enemy machine gun fired from the village. The pilot radioed "bingo" (out of fuel) and cut the line. The two men crashed to the ground. With keen insight and savvy skills, SSgt Edward Bartberger was credited with saving the lives of the critically wounded. The first platoon secured the RON site and ushered the wounded down the next morning.

For their actions on 14 December 1968; Sp. 4 John "Smitty" Smith (Medevaced to Japan) was awarded Purple Heart (PH); LT Fred Barbour, ARCOM/V, PH; LNO LT Bret Francis ARCOM/V, PH; and LNO Captain Givens given BS/V, PH. For selfless acts, above and beyond the call of duty, with complete disregard for his safety as he attempted to route the enemy and provide relief to nine wounded and trapped men, LT David Allen Lenchner was awarded the Purple Heart, posthumously.

Lt. D. A. Lenchner

Lt. David Allan Lenchner, 21, died Dec. 15 of wounds he received while in combat at Vietnam. He is the son of Mr. and Mrs. Irving Lenchner of 846 Hailshan Road, Newport News.

He was a graduate of Norview High School, Norfolk, and a member of St. Jerome's Catholic Church, Newport News. He was assigned to duty with Special Forces in Vietnam.

Besides his parents he is survived by one sister, Miss Phyliss Lenchner of Newport News; two brothers, Clifford E. Lenchner of Newport News; Joseph J. Lenchner of Venturia, Calif., his maternal grandparents, Mr. and Mrs. John Kempwicz of Wilkes Barre, Pa.

Funeral arrangements will be

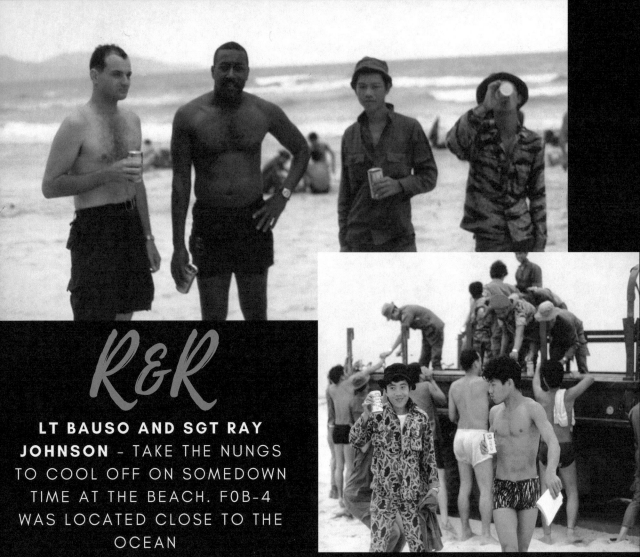

R&R

LT BAUSO AND SGT RAY JOHNSON – TAKE THE NUNGS TO COOL OFF ON SOMEDOWN TIME AT THE BEACH. FOB-4 WAS LOCATED CLOSE TO THE OCEAN

Chief Warrant Officer 2
Brian Devaney

On May 30, 1970, a U.S. Army helicopter UH-1H (tail number 67-17205) from the 170th Assault Helicopter Company was shot down during a SOG extraction in Laos. There are two accounts for this incident: First account - is CW2 Brian J. (B.J.) DeVaney of the 170th AHC, a native Canadian, whose last day of flying was the day before. One of his last missions was to insert a SOG recon team from CCC in the "Bra" area of the Ho Chi Minh Trail on May 28, 1970. On May 30th, he learned the team was now in trouble and need to be extracted from the area, he felt it was his responsibility to extract the team since he had inserted them and therefore took the mission. Upon the approach to extract the team, the helicopter came under intense fire from an RPD machine gun, raking the chopper from front to rear while it hovered to pick up the team under fire. Several rounds entered from the rear of the aircraft. Two rounds hit crew chief SP4 John P. Martin, sitting directly behind the pilot DeVaney, one round hit Martin in the left thigh, and one hit the left tibia and went through the right femur. One of these rounds that hit Martin passed through about a 1/4" inch crack in the armor plating protecting the pilot, hitting CWO DeVaney's armor chest plate and bouncing back into his heart killing him instantly. The aircraft rolled, crashed, and burned. SP4 Martin came to from being unconscious and found he was under the fuel cell of the aircraft. As he began to crawl away, LT John W Naurot, of CCC's Recon Team, left the safety of the bomb crater and retrieved Martin by pulling him into the crater. How the other crew members consisting of the co-pilot Taylor and B.J got to the crater is not clear, either the co-pilot and other members got to the crater themselves, or the other members of the Recon Team exposed themselves to the hail of bullets by crawling out and pulling the crew back to safety. One SCU scout was also KIA in this incident.

All members were rescued by another 170th Helicopter which lost 4" of the tail rotor in the extraction. (Information provided by John P. Martin and edited by Robert Noe) [Taken from macvsog.cc] Second account - LT Robert Talmadge, the 1st Lift Platoon leader, provides a lengthy description of the 'life and times in the 170th,' a description of B.J.'s flying skills, and details about his death in 'Unknown Warriors: Canadians in Vietnam' by Fred Gaffin. B.J. was born a Canadian and retained his Canadian citizenship. What follows is an extract of that account: B.J. had completed one year in gunships and was most of the way through his six-month extension. He was a well-respected slick aircraft commander. He had been shot down twice during his time with the 170th. He wasn't scheduled to fly on the 30th because he was due to go home. However, the night before he signed up for one more mission. On the 30th he was Flight Lead on an SOB extraction mission out of Dak To. Talmadge was flying co-pilot in the reserve ship which launched when the call came that 'Lead's down.' The recon team and downed crew were in a bomb crater surrounded by jagged tree stumps in an area of Laos called 'The Bra.' CW2 Rich Glover was the aircraft commander of Talmadge's aircraft. The recon team was receiving heavy machine-gun fire and didn't want any more helicopters to come into their area. Disregarding this, Rich made a high overhead approach and hovered near the edge of the crater. As soon as the downed crew and wounded recon team members were on board, Rich started backing away from the crater. He inadvertently hit a tree stump with the tail rotor but managed to maintain control of the aircraft. As they headed for Ben Het, Talmadge got out of his seat and went back to help CW2 Mike Taylor, who had been flying with B.J., and the other wounded. He yelled to Rich that they needed to get to the Evac Hospital in Pleiku. Rich yelled back that he didn't think the tail rotor would hold up that long but it did. Later inspection revealed almost three inches were missing from the tips of the tail rotor and one blade still had a four-inch piece of wood stuck in it. About 10 minutes after B.J. was taken into the Evac Hospital a nurse returned to say that B.J. didn't make it. A doctor later told them that a remnant from a large-caliber round had come through the side of B.J.'s chicken plate, bounced back into his body, and entered his heart. [Taken from vhpa.org].

Chief Warrant Officer 2 Brian Devaney

The 1969 battle at Dak To had been devastating on the 170th AHC in the way of manpower and equipment. Many were dead, more wounded, and a large amount of those surviving the carnage was rotating home. A feisty Warrant Officer, known for his courage and dedication to the mission of the Bikini Birds, extended for 6 months to assist in training new pilots to fly the unique missions with MACV-SOG into Laos and Cambodia. **CWO Brian J. DeVaney, BJ** as he was called, was an officer in the United States Army, but he was a Canadian by birth and citizenship. The friendly, but reserved young Warrant Officer, was born in Toronto, Canada, and though he had moved to the United States at a young age, he had retained his Canadian citizenship. He volunteered for the Army, volunteered for Vietnam, volunteered to fly SOG, and volunteered to extend his tour of duty for six months to assure new pilots flying for the 170th were properly trained. BJ was about to volunteer for the last time in his life.

The new men found him demanding and exacting in his training of them, to the point they often wondered if anything they did was right. BJ pointed out every indiscretion and immediately told them what needed to be done and how to do it. BJ was respected and loved, but often in his absence was called names he would never have cared to hear in person, by the pilots he trained, because of his demanding and exacting nature when it came to flying. Every one of those same pilots later admitted how BJ's demanding training, and exacting call for proficiency, allowed them to fly in ways they never thought themselves capable of. The same training they cursed him for, time and again, was to save their lives, the lives of their crew, and the lives of the men they carried.

The battles that took place at Dak Seang, in April of 1970, were a repeat of the Dak To battles of the year before. The 170th was once again cut to the bare bones in both aircraft and manpower. Those available to fly were tired, and some were burned out and unable to handle hot missions. While new men began pouring in to replace the dead and wounded, Pilots from the 57th AHC filled in vacant slots, being the only available pilots familiar with the 170th mission demands. In many ways, the 170th was a new unit again, with a handful of old-timers to train the new guys, and fly SOG missions.

On April 29th, Brian DeVaney stopped by the Operations Room on his way to the "O" Club for his nightly drink with friends. He was a short-timer, in fact, too short to fly. He had already been removed from the flight roster, pending shipment home to the states. For his last scheduled assignment, BJ had inserted a SOG team into the Bra area of southern Laos. During the insertion, they had taken heavy fire, and BJ was concerned over the team's status. In the Ops Room, BJ discovered the team had been making regular contact with the NVA and was set up alongside of the hill for the night, reporting movement around them. All the familiar signs were there for trouble. BJ entered his name on the next day's roster for the FOB group, as lead, and would be flying with CWO Mike Taylor. Having assured he would be there to extract the team, he felt responsible for, BJ went off to the club to enjoy his evening and talk about going back to the world.

The Bra was beyond a doubt the hottest operational area of the southern Laos assignments with SOG and had been since the SOG operations had commenced. The area was named "The Bra" for the distinctive shape of the river where Hwy 110 split to meet the Ho Chi Minh Trail. Hwy 96 which crossed The Bra was the main artery for supplies and troop movements for the NVA. The amount of activity in The Bra was so intensive, that everyone (aviator and ground teams alike) gritted their teeth when they drew it as a mission. The NVA's Binh Tram 37 was there (a major NVA base camp) to stockpile and ship supplies, arms, and ammunition to units in Vietnam via the trail. Stationed at the camp were security battalions, and the highly trained counter-recon hunter teams, whose sole mission was to hunt down and kill SOG reconnaissance teams. The entire Bra was saturated with fortified antiaircraft placements, and as early as 1968, Russian Mi-6 Helicopters had been seen in the area. Everyone went to The Bra when the mission dictated, but no one volunteered for The Bra. No one, that is, except BJ DeVaney.

Article credit "R.Noe, Studies and Observation Group, MACVSOG.CC: Tales from SOG"

Last Mission of Helicopter UH-1H 68-15262

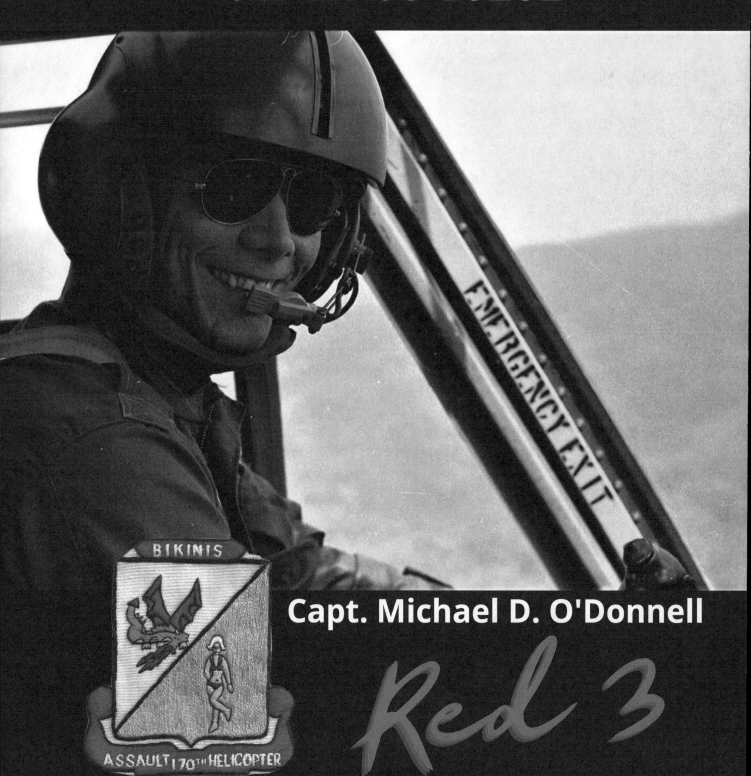

Capt. Michael D. O'Donnell

Red 3

BIKINIS

ASSAULT 170TH HELICOPTER

Crew of Helicopter UH-1H 68-15262

Ssgt Berman Ganoe JR

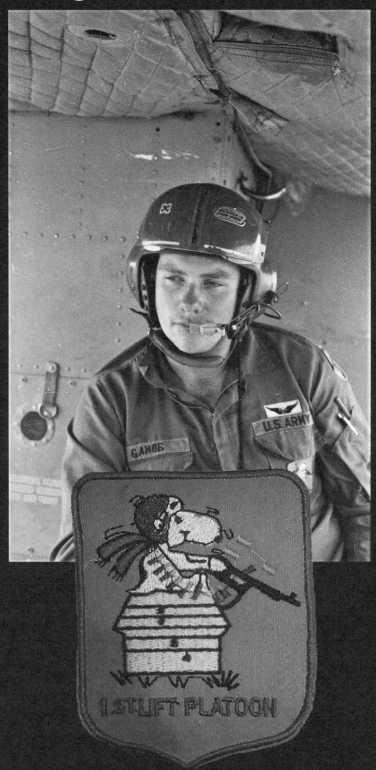

Ssgt Rudy Morales Becerra

CWO JOHN CHARLES HOSKEN

SOG RT Pennsylvania team members on Helicopter UH-1H 68-15262

SFC John Boronski   **SFC Gary Alan Harned**   **1LT Jerry Lynn Pool**

Including 5 unnamed indigenous troops of the Recon Team

Summary of Last Mission of Helicopter UH-1H 68-15262

Personnel in Incident: Rudy Morales Becerra; Berman Ganoe; John C. Hosken; Michael O'Donnell; John Boronski; Gary A. Harned, Jerry L. Pool (all missing) SYNOPSIS: Kontum, South Vietnam was home base to what was known as FOB2 (Forward Observation Base 2), classified, long-term operations of the Special Operations Group (SOG) that involved daily operations into Laos and Cambodia. SOG teams operated out of Kontum but staged out of Dak To. The mission of the 170th Assault Helicopter Company ('Bikinis') was to perform the insertion, support, and extraction of these SOG teams deep in the forest on 'the other side of the fence' (a term meaning Laos or Cambodia, where U.S. forces were not allowed to be based). Normally, the teams consisted of two 'slicks' (UH1 general purpose helicopters), two Cobras (AH1 assault helicopters), and other fighter aircraft which served as standby support. On March 24, 1970, helicopters from the 170th were sent to extract a MACV-SOG long-range reconnaissance patrol (LRRP) team which was in contact with the enemy about fourteen miles inside Cambodia in Ratanakiri Province. The flight leader, RED LEAD, serving as one of two extraction helicopters was commanded by James E. Lake. Capt. Michael D. O'Donnell was the aircraft commander of one of the two cover aircraft (serial #68-15262, RED THREE). His crew consisted of WO John C. Hoskins, pilot; SP4 Rudy M. Beccera, crew chief; and SP4 Berman Ganoe, gunner. The MACV-SOG team, Recon Team Pennsylvania, included 1LT Jerry L. Pool, team leader and team members SSG John A. Boronsky and SGT Gary A. Harned as well as five indigenous team members. The team had been in contact with the enemy all night and had been running and ambushing, but the hunter team pursuing them was relentless and they were exhausted and couldn't continue to run much longer.

When Lake and O'Donnell arrived at the team's location, there was no landing zone (LZ) nearby and they were unable to extract them immediately. The two helicopters waited in a high orbit over the area until the team could move to a more suitable extraction point. While the helicopters were waiting, they were in radio contact with the team. After about 45 minutes in orbit, Lake received word from LT Pool that the NVA hunter team was right behind them. RED LEAD and RED THREE made a quick trip to Dak To for refueling. RED THREE was left at a station in case of an emergency. When Lake returned to the site, Pool came over the radio and said that if the team wasn't extracted then, it would be too late. Capt. O'Donnell evaluated the situation and decided to pick them up. He landed on the LZ and was on the ground for about 4 minutes, and then transmitted that he had the entire team of eight on board. The aircraft was beginning its ascent when it was hit by enemy fire, and an explosion in the aircraft was seen. The helicopter continued in flight for about 300 meters, then another explosion occurred, causing the aircraft to crash in the jungle. According to Lake, bodies were blown out the doors and fell into the jungle. [NOTE: According to the U.S. Army account of the incident, no one was observed to have been thrown from the aircraft during either explosion.] The other helicopter crewmen were stunned. One of the Cobras, Panther 13, radioed 'I don't think a piece bigger than my head hit the ground.' The second explosion was followed by a yellow flash and a cloud of black smoke billowing from the jungle. Panther 13 made a second high-speed pass over the site and came under fire, but made it away unscathed. Lake decided to go down and see if there was a way to get to the crash site. As he neared the ground, he was met with intense ground fire from the entire area. He could not see the crash site since it was under heavy tree cover. There was no place to land, and the ground fire was withering.

He elected to return the extract team to Dak To before more aircraft were lost. Lake has carried the burden of guilt with him for all these years, and has never forgiven himself for leaving his good friend O'Donnell and his crew behind. The Army account concludes by stating that O'Donnell's aircraft began to burn immediately upon impact. Aerial search and rescue efforts began immediately; however, no signs of life could be seen around the crash site. Because of the enemy situation, attempts to insert search teams into the area were futile. SAR efforts were discontinued on April 18. Search and rescue teams who surveyed the site reported that they did not hold much hope for survival for the men aboard, but lacking proof that they were dead, the Army declared all 7 missing in action. Michael O'Donnell was recommended for the Congressional Medal of Honor for his actions on March 24, 1970. He was awarded the Distinguished Flying Cross, the Air Medal, the Bronze Star, and the Purple Heart as well as promoted to the rank of Major following his loss incident. O'Donnell was highly regarded by his friends in the 'Bikinis.' They knew him as a talented singer, guitar player, and poet. One of his poems has been widely distributed, but few understand that the author remains missing. "If you are able, save them a place inside of you and save one backward glance when you are leaving for the places they can no longer go. Be not ashamed to say you loved them, though you may or may not have always. Take what they have left and what they have taught you with their dying and keep it with your own. And in that time when men decide and feel safe to call the war insane, take one moment to embrace those gentle heroes you left behind." Major Michael Davis O'Donnell 1 January 1970 Dak To, Vietnam [Taken from vhpa.org; a much longer and more detailed account of the extraction attempt is found at the same website]

Location of crash site in Cambodia Loss Coordinates:

142750N 1071816E (YB484003)

Major Michael Davis O'Donnell
1 January 1970
Dak To, Vietnam

I have tasted the air in the early morning,

before the sun and before the day...

I have let it run all down my face and stain my clothes

and I have learned to wash myself with the part of the day that remains...

I am drying in the sun at Dak To.

I am each day becoming less interested in the way the morning tastes

and I am drying in the sun at Dak To...

I am dying in the sun at Dak To.

March 18, 1970

Michael Davis O'Donnell

To read more of Major Michael O'Donnell poetry research the book -In That Time: Michael O'Donnell and the Tragic Era of Vietnam

THE RATS

OF

Khe Sanh

By Bob Donoghue

s 1968 began to unfold, SOGS Forward Operating Base #3 (FOB-3 located on the Southeastern perimeter of the Khe Sanh Combat Base began to switch from offensive to defensive operations. As the enemy intensified their direct fire into the base, more and more time and effort was spent digging and building extensive trench and bunker complexes. Constructed sandbags, lumber, and aluminum pallets. These semi-subterranean complexes soon became home to two kids of rats. Two-legged fatigue-wearing men known as "The Rats of Khe Sahn."

HF ELDORADO

FOB-3, Khe Sanh, Left to Right: Kyle Buchanan, Kara Garland, Ful   n Moore, Bob Donoghue, Gary Matson who later was KIA

Khe Sanh's rats lived in the sandbagged bunker structures feeding off the remains of discarded C ration cans. As nighttime approached, they would emerge from their nests to scurry about the area. Anyone trying to get sleep at one time or another had one of these critters run across their body. During this time, several people were bitten and had to undergo an extremely painful series of rabies shots.

The tide slowly turned against these rats due to the deteriorating weather conditions and the North Vietnamese Army. The only way to supply the troops with food and ammunition was parachute drops. After several days of enemy fire and lousy flying weather, the resupply drops tapered off creating a shortage of food.

 Bru Montagnards supplement their
lack of rations with rats at Khe Sahn
FOB-3 1968

Our indigenous troops, the Bru Montagnard's, soon devised a plan to supplement their meager rations. First they would take a small individual equipment net an would stretch it across the bottom half of a trench. They would then have two other men start beating on the bunker sandbags with pieces of two by fours. The rats, being startled by the banging, would scurry out of the bunker and down the trench to be entangled within the net. A short time later the Bru would be heating up the water in a #10 can with pieces of C-4 explosive and throwing the captured rats into the can to cook them.These Khe Sanh rodents provided fine dining at the time when rations were limited. As the siege progressed it became harder for the Bru to find these fine tasting rodents.....

Bob Donghue

On October 30, 1968, SGT Gary L. Matson of forwarding Operating Base 1, Command and Control North (CCN), MACV-SOG, was installing mines in the Mai Loc launch site mine field with fellow SOG member Jeffrey Junkins when SGT Matson accidentally tripped a "Bouncing Betty" anti-personnel mine which killed him instantly. Junkins landed on a mine and it took several hours before he was able to be pulled him from the minefield. (Note: Jeffrey Junkins was not killed in Vietnam, but he was just as much a victim of his experience there causing his death by suicide on May 19, 1999) [Taken from macvsog.cc]

Navy Seals in MACV SOG

Recon and Naval Advisory Detachment

Part 1

Shadduck seen on left with a Seal Team

Navy Seals were immersed into MACV-SOG on a variety of levels but in recon there was a very limited amount. Gary Shadduck is one of only 6 that joined the ranks of **SOG** recon. Details are limited to Shadduck's military service which is surprising as he completed 6 tours of duty in Vietnam a lot of that time was with Seal team 1. In 1966 Shadduck signs up for a 6mth tour with **SOG** (Seal's in **SOG** could only sign up for 6 mths stints) He joined Recon Team Colorado his team mates were Ted Braden, Jim Hetrick, J.D Bath, Allan Keller, Lt George Sisler, Gerald Howland, Donald Brown. He rejoined SEAL Team one, after SOG. From February 69- July 69 he was a PRU advisor in the Can Tho area from Feb 69 - July 69. Shadduck would return to SEAL Team one in 1970 as an advisor to the LDNN (South Vietnamese SEALS) . There he taught sabotage techniques ,Underwater Demolitions, Explosive Ordnance Disposal and Boat Support to be used in the North at Haiphong Harbor and other high value targets above the 17th parallel in the North Vietnam.

**Richard Ray - From Seal Team one would join RT OHIO
August 66 - November 66 After he would return to Seal Team one.**

In the early days of the Navy Seal's involvement in the Vietnam war they were focused on training South Vietnamese Commandos in an effort to target North Vietnamese sites of interest. During these early days American troops could not travel past the 17th parallel. The South Vietnamese would travel the rest of the journey on their own, in high speeds boats (Nasty Boats a Norwegian 80-foot Nasty Class patrol boat) These were under the umbrella of Operation 34 A. The code name for these operations was Nautilus. In July 1962 C.I.A. control of these operations would cease MACV SOG would take over. Now part of Joint unconventional warfare task force (JUWTF) who would plan covert blacks ops.

Chief Quartermaster Cunningham - Had extensive military service with the U.S Navy. He was a Korean war vet with the UDT the predecessor of the SEALS. In August 66 Cunningham would take the 1-1 spot of RT IOWA of **MACV SOG** and stayed with the team until November 66. After he returned to his SEAL team. Then a PRU advisor.
July 69 - Jan 70 in Vinh Long.
Cunningham would stay in the U.S. Navy until his retirement in 1972. Research shows that both Seal team members on SOG Recon teams (Ray and Cunningham) both served at same time.

- **Romeo Platoon, SEAL Team One**
- (Jan 1971 - ___) LT Tom Boyhan and LTJG Stephan Dundas
- **Chief Dever Cunningham**
- TM1 Lester Moe (KIA- 29 March 71)
- ETN2 William Woodruff
- ETN2 John Brooks
- ETN2 Bill Ferrand
- Kenny Meyer
- HM1 Bob Sell
- TM1 Lester Moe (Killed 1971 at Rach Soi)
- Joe Murray
- Jim Werder
- Clay Sherman

Cunningham 1-1 and fellow RT Iowa team mate Leonard W. Tilley 1-0

After his 6mth stint with RT Iowa Cunningham would serve with the PRU (Provincial Reconnaissance Unit) in an advisory role. It was common to find Navy Seals in this role with the PRU but not exclusive to them, 5th Special forces were also active in the same position. Most advisors were very experienced combat soldiers. PRU activities during the Vietnam war are still controversial to this day. Intelligence was gathered through Operation Phoenix, the CIA, and a variety of other sources. The PRU was then sent out to capture or neutralize verified targets, who were key figures in raising funds or supporting VC operations against American or South Vietnamese forces.

Lieutenant O-3, U.S. Navy Michael Collins - Unrestricted Line Officer Surface Warfare was born on October 12, 1942, in Concord, California. He entered the U.S. Naval Academy in May 1960 and was commissioned an Ensign in the U.S. Navy on June 3, 1964. Ensign Collins then remained at the Academy in training for the U.S. Olympic Swimming Team, and served as an instructor in the Academy's Physical Education Department from June to September 1964. He next attended the Combat Information Center Watch Officers course at U.S. Fleet Anti-Air Warfare Training Center San Diego, California, from October to November 1964, followed by service as a CIC Officer aboard the destroyer leader USS John S. McCain (DL-3) from December 1964 to May 1966. LtJg Collins attended Underwater Demolition Team Replacement Accession training with Class 039 at NAB Coronado, California, from May to November 1966, and then served with Underwater Demolition Team ELEVEN (UDT-11) at NAB Coronado from November 1966 to June 1968. His next assignment was with the **Studies and Observations Group** under the U.S. Military Assistance Command Vietnam from June 1968 to July 1969, followed by service with SEAL Team ONE at NAB Coronado from July 1969 until he was killed in action while deployed to South Vietnam on March 4, 1971. Michael Collins was buried at Fort Rosecrans National Cemetery in San Diego, California.

Robert J. Fay Commander O-5, U.S. Navy

Robert Fay was born on January 30, 1924, in Boston, Massachusetts. He entered the United States Merchant Marine on August 28, 1942, and served on ships in both the Atlantic and Pacific Thea. CDR Fay served as Commanding Officer of the Navy EOD Facility at Indian Head from March 1961 to August 1962, and then as Commanding Officer of the destroyer USS Johnston (DD-821) from September 1962 to June 1964. His next assignment was as Commander of a deployed detachment of Naval Operations Support Group Atlantic from July to September 1964, and then as Chief of Staff of Naval Operations Support Group Atlantic at Naval Station Norfolk from October 1964 to March 1965. CDR Fay's final assignment was as Officer in Charge of the U.S. **Naval Advisory Detachment** in Da Nang, South Vietnam Ban Dao Son Tra (Monkey Mountain) Da Nang, SOG Ops 31. Part of the clandestine Studies and Observations Group with U.S. Military Assistance Command from April 1965 until he was killed in action during a mortar attack on October 28, 1965. Robert Fay was buried at Arlington National Cemetery. He was the first United States Navy SEAL to be killed in action, although not the first to die on an actual combat mission. For his full military history please go to http://veterantributes.org/TributeDetail.php?recordID=2099

photo credit main photo navy seal museum

Navy Seal Lt. Thomas R. Norris (NAD) and Nguyen Van Kiet, the Vietnamese Sea Commando

Lt. Thomas Norris and Nguyen Van Kiet, the Vietnamese Sea Commando who accompanied Norris on the rescues of Clark and Hambleton. They were assigned to MACV-SOG Danang Naval Advisory Detachment (NAD) Lt. Thomas R. Norris would be awarded the Medel of Honour for this mission and Kiet the Navy Cross the highest award the Navy can give a foreign national.

Holding an AK-47, South VN Navy SEAL (LDNN) Nguyen Van Kiet searches an NVA tank that was abandoned near the Mieu Giang river during search and Rescue Operations for BAT-21 Bravo in April 1972

VN Navy SEAL(LDNN) Nguyen Van Kiet was awarded the Navy Cross.

For conspicuous gallantry and intrepidity in action at the risk of his life above and beyond the call of duty while serving as a SEAL Advisor with the Strategic Technical Directorate Assistance Team, Headquarters, U.S. Military Assistance Command, Vietnam. During the period 10 to 13 April 1972, Lieutenant Norris completed an unprecedented ground rescue of two downed pilots deep within the heavily controlled enemy territory in Quang Tri Province. Lieutenant Norris, on the night of 10 April, led a five-man patrol through 2,000 meters of heavily controlled enemy territory, located one of the downed pilots at daybreak, and returned to the Forward Operating Base (FOB). On 11 April, after a devastating mortar and rocket attack on the small FOB, Lieutenant Norris led a three-man team on two unsuccessful rescue attempts for the second pilot. On the afternoon of the 12th, a Forward Air Controller located the pilot and notified Lieutenant Norris. Dressed in fisherman's disguises and using a sampan, Lieutenant Norris and one Vietnamese travelled throughout that night and found the injured pilot at dawn. Covering the pilot with bamboo and vegetation, they began the return journey, successfully evading a North Vietnamese patrol. Approaching the FOB, they came under heavy machine gun fire. Lieutenant Norris called in an air strike which provided suppression fire and a smoke screen, allowing the rescue party to reach the FOB. By his outstanding display of decisive leadership, undaunted courage, and selfless dedication in the face of extreme danger, Lieutenant Norris enhanced the finest traditions of the United States Naval Service.

Bat 21 Bravo

AKA

LTC Iceal Hambleton

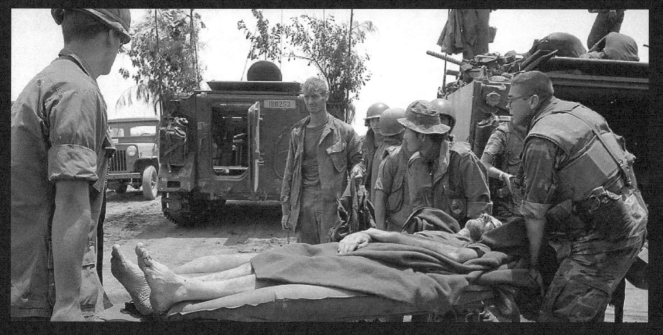

1972: Lieutenant Thomas Norris stands in the background at center as Lieutenant Colonel Iceal Hambleton (on the stretcher), a United States Air Force navigator and electronic warfare officer who was shot down over South Vietnam during the 1972 Easter Offensive, is taken to a waiting M113 armored personnel carrier to be evacuated. Norris was tasked with mounting a ground operation to recover Lt. Col. Hambleton, 1st Lt. Mark Clark, and 1st Lt. Bruce Walker from behind enemy lines. Norris, along with Vietnamese commando Nguyễn Văn Kiệt, successfully brought out two of the three downed airmen from more than 1.2 miles behind enemy lines. (U.S. Dept. of Defense)

Dennis K McCormack
Seal Team 1
Advisor - (NAD)

Inspired by the movie "The Navy Frogman," Dennis joined the US Navy in 1959 and became a UDT Frogman. Recognized as a capable operator, he was called up to become plank owner, one of the first 60 men assigned to SEAL Team One when it was first formed in 1962. Dennis' duties as a SEAL involved rigorous training and operational activities in several European countries, preparations for the Cuban Missile Crisis in 1962, and a combat tour in Vietnam in 1964 "I was an RM1-P1 in 1963 and was leading Petty Officer for 37A ops out of DaNang in 1964, **Bob Wagner** was a good friend and I, relieved him at DaNang in 1964."

McCormack with team of Nungs circa 1964, DaNang, Vietnam OP34A (NAD)

Briefing Nungs by Marble Mountain circa 1964.

Nungs were a large part of the Sea Commandos which then went North of the 17th parallel via Nasty Class boats.

Dennis K McCormack Seal Team 1 Advisor-OP34A (NAD) Training a (Sea Commando)Vietnamese Frogman in demolition tactics Danang 1964

Dennis K McCormack

Dec.31.1938 -April.14.2020

The author was deployed to Vietnam in 1964. Initially briefed in Saigon, and after depositing all identification, medical records, etc., with the Studies and Observation Group **(SOG)**, and after receiving DoD false identification documentation cards, as well as khaki unmarked clothing, and civilian clothes, we were sent to DaNang and our camp just across the bay on the beach called My Khe.

Stronger: Develop the Resilience You Need to Succeed By George Everly Jr., Dr. Douglas Strouse and Dr. Dennis K. McCormack

LTJG. Jim Hawes

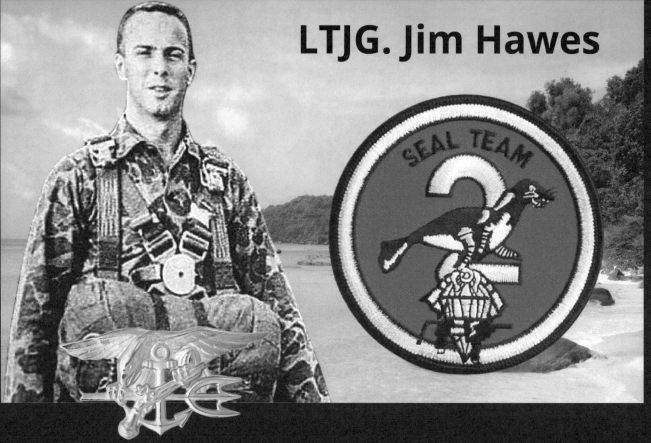

Hawes was one of 2 Seal officers that arrived in Danang from April, 1964— April, 1965 The other officer was Lieutenant Commander Ken Wolfe. He was was Commanding Officer of UDT-21, when he got his orders to stand up MACV/SOG/NAD. Both men where there to oversea the transfer from the CIA to the DOD (US Military). Adding to the assignment was the building up of the frequency and intensity of OPS north of the 17th Parallel using Nasty Class boats carrying South Vietnamese Sea commandos.

Hawes would go on to further covert ops throughout the world including Africa where his men narrowing missed Che Guevara in the Congo. At this point he was a CIA contractor. He wrote a book about some of his military career including his time Vietnam which is chapter 3 in his book "Cold War Navy SEAL" by Jim Hawes

"Cold War Navy SEAL gives unprecedented insight into a clandestine chapter in US history through the experiences of Hawes, a distinguished Navy frogman and later a CIA contractor. His journey began as an officer in the newly-formed SEAL Team 2, which then led him to Vietnam in 1964 to train hit-and-run boat teams who ran clandestine raids into North Vietnam. Those raids directly instigated the Gulf of Tonkin Incident".

Lt. Cmdr Lloyd F.Tayor
A.K.A

Jose Taylor

Ho Van Ky Thoai Commander of CCSS and NAD pins a medal on Lt.Cmdr. Lloyd F. Taylor

OBITUARIES

A.K.A. Jose Taylor (SEAL)
Lloyd F. Taylor

Retired Lt. Cmdr. Lloyd F. Taylor, U.S. Navy, who was lovingly known as Joe "Jose" Taylor, age 79, of Crestview, Fla., passed away Friday, Oct. 14, 2005, at his home.

He was born in St. Joseph, Mo., on July 23, 1926, and lived in Crestview for the past 15 years. Joe was a veteran of the U.S. Navy who served in World War II with the Scouts and Raiders, in Korea with the UDT, and a Plank Owner of Seal Team II, commanding officer USS Stallion ATA-193, and Operations Officer at NAD Da Nang and MACV.SOG for two tours in Vietnam.

He is survived by his wife of 14½ years, Mary Elizabeth Taylor of Crestview; son, Patrick Taylor of Peyton, Colo.; daughters, Dr. Bonnie Taylor of San Mateo, Calif., Dr. Candice Subhiyah of Philadelphia, and Dawn Taylor of Lakeland, Fla.; four grandchildren, Laurel, Blair, Camaren and Alexander; two beloved sons-in-law, Lee Cohen and Dr. Raja Subhiyah; lots of loving cousins; and two aunts, Estella May Miller and Crystal Adkins in Savannah, Miss.

Joe will be interred at Arlington National Cemetery at a later date.

He will be dearly missed.

Whitehurst-Powell Funeral Home is entrusted with arrangements.

SK1 ROBERT KAY WAGNER

7 Tours in Vietnam

August 31, 1963 - February 27, 1964 - Naval
Advisory Detachment

September 14, 1964 - February 25, 1965 -
NAD, Da Nang

June 12, 1965 - November 27, 1965 -
Detachment Golf (Nha Be)

March 12, 1966 - September 7, 1966 -
Detachment Delta (Nha Be)

October 20, 1966 - June 15, 1967 - Vung Tau
(Provincial Reconnaissance Unit Training Facility)

June 30 1968 - August 15, 1968 - Advisory Team 57
(TraVinh, Vinh Binh Province)

**Wagner training Training
Vietnamese frogmen Danang**

On June 28, 1968, Bob deployed to Viet Nam and reported to Tra Vinh in Vinh Binh Province where he operated with his PRU team. According to his last letter he sent home (August 13, 1968) his PRU team was really hurting the VC (".... the bastards are hanging on by their teeth in this province"). Helen received this letter after being notified about her husband's death.
Late in the evening on August 15, 1968 Bob and his PRU team were moving toward a Viet Cong held village in the Cang Long district of Vinh Binh Province. According to letters (from LTC. Ralph W. Girdner and Lt. Thomas Nelson) sent to Bob's wife, approximately 200 meters from the hamlet two Viet Cong (VC) spotted the team's movement and ran toward the village. Bob's interpreter tried to run down the VC, however he tripped a booby trap and the subsequent explosion killed the interpreter and Bob instantly. Two SEALs, George Davis and John Lynch, carried Bob out of the area to a helicopter which took Bob to the 3rd Surgical Field Hospital in Dong Tam. Nothing could be done for him due to shrapnel wounds to the head and chest.

CHIEF PETTY OFFICER (SEAL)
ROBERT F SULLIVAN

March 26, 1931 ~ April 25, 2019)

My second tour of Vietnam was in 1964 at NAD (Naval Advisory Detachment, MACV SOGs Naval division) DaNang South Vietnam.

On January 24 President Lyndon Johnson signed OPLAND 34A that authorized US Personnel to assume the previous work of SOG CIA Vietnam under the new SOG MACV Commanded by General William Westmorland. With this directive the military takes over the counterinsurgency war, and I'm back in uniform in Vietnam. (In Cammies) NAD DaNang would be the US Navy's headquarters of SOG MACV in its assisting the South Vietnam Government in resisting the war with North Vietnam by aggressive acts across the 17th parallel by Commandoes trained by US Navy SEALs.

We operated from an expanded site from where Don Raymond and I had set up training for operation Vulcan (SOG OP34A) in 1962. It was now a group of five separate training sites spread out along 4 or 5 miles of beach. The Headquarters was on the northern end of the beach, and that was where the SEAL advisors were housed. Each site was separated and segregated to keep the personnel from contact with each other for security reasons. Each site was designated for a specific mission. SEAL personnel were assigned to train a particular group of agents for their mission and only that mission. Usually, there were two SEALs assigned to each group, but in a few cases it took up to four. We had graduated from operating from Junks to "Swift Boats", and then to the "Nasties" (Norwegian Attack Craft). This was a definite improvement in our speed and armament capability. All the boats were heavily armed.

Since Don Raymond my partner on my first tour decided to leave the Navy for Commercial Diving, I was partnered up with a 1st class Bos'n mate named Ray Abreu. Ray came to the SEALs after four years in UDT-11 and about four years of shipboard duty. Ray was what you would call a tough guy. He was a good athlete and hard as nails. We were going to get along fine and pull off some good ops. Our group of agents came from the remaining Vietnamese trained in Taiwan for the Vietnamese UDT Team, but not chosen for the First "Vulcan" operation. There were twenty of them. There was also an interpreter in the group. He was a noncombatant and used only to explain our English to the group, and they're Vietnamese to us. We held a short course with the group on what American Commands they must know immediately without the need of an interpreter. We didn't want the need for an interpreter if we were in the middle of a firefight.

Warriors of all ethnic backgrounds must learn to listen to the leader, and understand his direct commands or they won't last very long. Our agents were in good physical condition, so getting them into good physical condition, so getting them into a condition to operate was not a problem. We were training these guys for Commando-type insertions into North Vietnam to destroy seaside Radar stations that tracked our shipping and aircraft and were used as a warning element to their approach into North Vietnam. There were numerous small mobile Radar and Surface to Air (SAM) missile sites tracking our Aircraft launched from Carriers in the Gulf of Tonkin. Because of the mountainous terrain of North Vietnam, the Seaside Radar sites picked up our aircraft flying even at low altitudes. Since small boat traffic was normal along the coast, our Swift Boats could get into IBS (Rubber Boat) launching range at night without trouble, and the Commando raids were successful in eliminating some of the sites and it reminded North Vietnam that we could cross their borders too. Small Electric power plants were also a seaside target. They use seawater to cool the oil-burning generators used to power military sites, and some of the more modern villages of North Vietnam. These sites were well camouflaged from aircraft and were not a high-priority target during early bombing raids.

Besides the normal water skills that our Frogs must have, we've incorporated small arms and demolition use into their training. Skills in the 3.5 rocket launchers, 40 mm grenade weapons, and 60 mm machine guns were added to the M-16 (AR 15) general use military weapon. An over-the-beach raiding party could consist of a Swift Boat, two rubber IBS (Inflatable Boat Small)with crews of 7 men each, and 6 gunners manning the Swift Boats 50 cal machine guns and 81 mm Mortars, plus act as backups to the raiding crews. The Swift Boat had a Coxswain and an Engineer that were not part of the Vietnamese Agent group. The Coxswain and Engineer were leftover contracts personnel from the SOG CIA days.

They were Scandinavian Merchant Seamen contracted by the CIA for their Navigational skills and used for their deniability of presence to the

International Control Committee (They were not Americans if captured) they were training their replacements from the Vietnamese Navy, because their contracts would end in December 1964. The CIA would always deny any American involvement in any covert clandestine operations because that's what the CIA always does. Just part of the job.

The Swift boats were a giant leap from the days when motorized fishing Junks were used to land clandestine agents across the 17th parallel into North Vietnam. The speed and armament of the Swift boats would better match them with the Swatow Gun Boats the North used, and the Junks the Swift boats replaced. The Swift Boats were 50 ft in length and powered with two V1271 GM diesel engines. (A Greyhound Bus is powered by a single 671 GM diesel engine) They had a range of 750 mi at 10 knots and a top speed of 32 knots. They could outrun a Swatow (28 km) North Vietnam's premier Gunboat. They had twin 50 cal machine guns mounted over the pilot house and a combination 50 cal machine gun and 81 mm Lanier fired mortar mounted on the stern. There was a 60 mm machine gun on the bow. They could carry 20 troops with a minimum crew of six. Two inflatable boats (IBS) could be launched from the stern area. The Boat had Radar for night operations and a fathometer for shallow water ops.

The typical op was to approach the target to within a few hundred yards at night, launch two IBS with 7 man-raiding parties each to land on the beach as clandestinely as possible. Destroy the target and egress by IBS to the Swift boat. The armament on the Swift boat can cover the egress and make the pickup in a relative manner close to shore. The Swift boat will use its speed and armaments as protection from Patrol boats. Being homeported in DaNang, the Swift boats have a possible range of 300 miles into North Vietnam. The loss of US bombing aircraft by SAM missiles, from the Radar- SAM sites, made the sites prime targets for over-the-beach raids.

The sites were generally mobile, but stationary at night. They were protected by armed militia from their immediate areas, with a few regular Army in supervision. The use of the militia as guards was proven to be a poor decision since many of them were asleep when a raiding party was coming ashore. To many of the local populations along the coast, their life was fishing, and the war was something happening far away. Time in the militia was something the government required along with their duty to make a living. It's the Communist way of life. Militias were poorly trained and during some raids, they ran rather than engage while protecting their assigned station. By March 1964 we had our troops ready for a real raid. We had been practicing on the other training sites with everything but live ammo. Ray and I felt confident in our Commandos. Then politics reared its ugly head. The powers that be decided that a Vietnamese Navy Lieutenant should command their first cross-border operation. Not as a raiding party participant but in command of the Swift Boat. We were not to go because at this time American involvement was still being denied. As our boss, Irish Flynn said "Just say aye-aye, and pull the rope " The raid was scheduled for a power station that was about 110 miles north of DaNang. The building had been well camouflaged but under the scrutiny from air photos the intake and return water lines from the ocean gave it away. The heated water from the return line was causing a stirred-up area in the water where it returned into the ocean. The water was crystal clear except for a spot directly offshore from one of the buildings built along the ocean side, and then fifty feet away from the same building a cable emerges from the ground and runs to a row of poles leading to the village. Two days later the Swift Boat returns and reports that the Raid had been aborted. The Vietnamese Navy Lieutenant had reasons for the abort that I was never privy to. Then through a conversation, we had at a bar in DaNang over a few beers, the Coxswain of the boat said that in his opinion the Lieutenant " Chickened Out"

This was the same problem SOG Combined Studies had with agents scheduled for Air Inserts (Parachuted) back in 1962-63. This was cured when US Personnel were made Jumpmasters and the deniability clause was ignored. Don and I were involved on one of those missions in 1962. This became a problem with Maritime operations, and the same cure was used, only without the knowledge of MACV until after President Johnson signed the Tonkin Gulf Initiative. Then the US Personal were legally released from the deniability restrictions. Our boss realized the problem was political from the get-go. We were not involved at our level but there was constant turmoil in the upper levels at the United States and the Vietnamese Headquarters. To shove an untrained Officer into the command of the type of warriors that we trained was asinine. Shipboard officers have no experience in commando-type operations. The Lieutenant remained with our Commando Team, but after some heated discussions between his superiors and our superiors, he was made a liaison officer. True to the French influence on the Vietnamese Navy, The Lieutenant would not live with his assigned team, but lived in quarters for other Vietnamese officers set aside in our compound (Trainees to operate the Swift Boats and Nasties) SEAL Team officers always lived with their platoons while in Vietnam. The only time they stayed in separate quarters was aboard US Naval Vessels and on US Military Bases. We went on to have several what we called successful operations with Ray and me running the show. Since Ray and I did not go ashore with the raiding parties, our best assessment was when the demolitions that were planted went off "High Order" and our personnel returned to the boat. We did have several casualties and two KIA, but none were left behind. On several trips, we were fired on by North Vietnam patrol boats that we assumed were Swatows. They gave up the chase shortly after we returned fire so we don't know if we scored some hits or we were just too fast for them. We were not foolish enough to continue to engage an unknown vessel because if it was a Swatow, we would have been severely outgunned.

On the plans made up by the high-paid plan makers, each site was to be bombed immediately following a raid, supposedly when it was without defenses. That old deniability crap went out the window when we wanted to be sure of getting a job done. (I'm sure I got some good licks in with our 50 calibers) We used API Ammo (Armor Piercing Incendiaries) and at night you can light up a target.

The North Vietnamese did not broadcast their losses, so our successes were often conjectured. Then again we were far down the information system, what we did hear was not taken as gospel since too much of the news was exaggerated to inflate the morale of our troops. All I know for sure is that we were part of a mission that was awarded the "Presidential Unit Citation" the country's highest award for combat and second only to the "Congressional Medal of Honor". I returned home a month before the other members of our deployment to bury my Mother who succumbed to cancer. Not a very happy homecoming.

There are a few things that stand out about my second tour that are vivid after all these years. One was the futility of trying to learn the Vietnamese language from someone out of touch with the people's language that we would use.

I'm daily reminded of a gash to my scalp by the scar on my bald dome when I look in a mirror. It happened while we were on a training run on a practice beach. The Swift boat ran aground on a submerged sandbar while making a high-speed turn in shallow water. The stop was so abrupt that I was thrown into the overhead of the pilot house.

When I returned to the Compound Doc Williams our corpsman sewed me up with baseball stitches and a can of spray that freezes the area long enough that you don't feel pain but you grit your teeth on each pull of the needle as he weaves his stitches into your bare head. I was O.K.

the next day, but you really bleed when you receive a wound to your head. Since it was not inflicted by a hostile act, "NO PURPLE HEART"! I've since heard of an LTJG that received three "P.H"s in the span of three months from scratches he got while crewing on Swift Boats(No gunshots), and he took advantage of the trip home rule if you receive three "P.H"s during a cruise to VN. He also received a "Silver Star" and "Bronze Star" and all this with less than four months' time spent in the country. I heard where he went on to do bigger and better things in our government. He became a Senator and almost our President. AH! The things that get arranged at the Officers Clubs. Another bloody evening I remember was when we thought the V. C. was testing out the integrity of the farthest camp south on our beach. The individual sites maintained their security and made up their guard assignments. Each site usually kept two guards on duty every night rotating the assignments every two hours. This particular site was the largest of the five sites and had a group of about 30 Chinese Nungs in training. The Nungs are an ethnic group that lives in Vietnam but immigrated from mainland China after WW II. They fought on the side of the French during the war with the Viet Minh 1946-54 (Indochina War) where they were considered mercenaries. Their language is a mixture of Chinese and Thai. We used Nungs to act as our security at the Main Compound where we lived. Many of the Special Forces Compounds throughout Vietnam used Nungs as security. The number one reason was that the VC had not infiltrated their communities like they had the Vietnamese. Nungs were known for their integrity to whoever paid them, and in Vietnam that was the U.S.

Throughout Vietnam, the VC would probe military compounds at night to get an idea if the site had security. If the security was lax or nonexistent they would do a "Snatch and Grab" of equipment and supplies, or just cause some harassment to provoke and frighten the occupants. In some cases, the whole area would be overrun if the resistance to a probe was low. This happened to a Special forces camp in our general area when Don Raymond and I were training our "Vulcan" crew here in 1962. This night the VC picked the wrong site to see if the troops would panic under attack. Some of the Nungs at that site were previously signed up to work for SOG CIA and were former mercenaries for the French in the war with the Viet Minh. Now they were working for SOGMACV but being paid by the CIA (Known as Combined Studies because the term CIA was not supposed to be used), these Nungs were tough cookies, and experienced fighters.

The main compound was hooked up to each site by radio, and phone line, plus each site had very pistols to fire colored flares in case of an attack or to light up the perimeter to make it a killing field. White flares were used periodically by site security to check the area surrounding the site. A series of red flares was a call for help, that the site was being probed or under attack. Each Training site had at least two vehicles. A Jeep, and a duce and a half truck for hauling personnel and equipment to the piers used by the Swift Boats and Nasties, plus for other uses. Ray and I were assigned a jeep our for work and personal use, this made us very independent.

The night the VC probed training site 5 #, we were hanging out in the main compound having a few at our Lounge/ Meeting Room which was SOP when not out on a operation, training, or in DaNang. The main camp had two guard towers manned by Nungs, and just before midnight they were shouting about the Red Flares going off down the beach. There were 8 to 10 SEALs in the compound at the time and all but the duty man loaded up our vehicles and went roaring down the beach. Ray and I were in the 1st jeep heading towards site number 5 #. We each had an AR 15 with a lot of ammo. Our own site was number 4 # and as we passed it on the way to 5 # we saw our guys were manning their sandbagged fighting holes. The Nungs of 5 # were in their fighting holes and firing into the expanse of no man's land to the south of the site. Not a steady fire on full automatic, but periodically from different places on the line as they were trained to do. The incoming fire ceased soon after we arrived so we surmised that it was only a probe. There were two casualties, one being the "No 1" man among the Nungs (The Leader) He had been shot through the neck, and bleed to death in a manner of minutes. The other Nung had a head wound and would survive. Both had been in a guard tower which lead us to believe that they were shot by a Sharpshooter (Sniper) since theirs were the first shots fired. There was other incoming fire from the area to the south of the site, but none of it hit anyone. The leader was probably checking up on the guard, or checking with him on something the guard had seen or heard from the tower, this being the reason why there were the two of them in the tower.

The sites would stay on the alert throughout the night, and in the AM there would be a group of anxious Nungs and SEALs ready to go south for VC hunting. It was common practice for the VC to collect their casualties and slip back into the hinterland, but an inspection of the area could tell us the approximate size of the attacking party, and maybe this time they might have left some dead behind. None were left behind, but by the appearance of the area directly south of the training site, there had been possibly 20 VCs in the probe.

The tracks in the sand (this was all beach area), and the spent cartridges gave us a fair guess at the size of the VC group. There were trails of blood so the Nungs got in some possible kills in the firefight. The area for the training sites and south of the training sites for 7-8 miles to the huge bump called "Marble Mountains" is a strip of beach and sand dunes continuing inland from the beach ¾ of a mile to a river. Just before the "Marble Mountains" the river bends inland and goes off into strictly

VC country all the way to the Laos border.

Our Nungs wanted to hunt down the VC responsible for the death of their Leader, but calmer heads prevailed. Mixing it up with the VC were

not what these guys were being trained to do, so it was turned over to the "I Corp" The Headquarters of ARVN (Vietnamese Army), and it caused our security to be ramped up a little, for one thing, SEALs started taking a weapon with them when they were in the lounge/meeting room. We had to rush back to our barracks for weapons before our charge off to do battle with the VC when the 5 # site was probed. The word came down that ARVN had found no VC in their search south to the Marble Mountains. My guess is that ARVN didn't get off the road in their search. In 1964 before US advisors were stationed with the ARVN units, they didn't go looking for a fight with the VC. A year later after my return to CONUS, Special Forces (Green Berets) found a complete VC stronghold dug into a maze of tunnels in the Marble Mountains. There are five large out cropping's that in the Vietnamese language translate to "Mountains made from Marble" They estimated there was a Battalion of hardcore VC involved. They even had a hospital. It was realized through interrogation of prisoners that the place had been there from the days of the French occupation, and had been a place used by the Viet Minh against the French. It took The US Marines that made their first landing in Vietnam just south of the NAD training sites in 1965 to take over the Marble Mountain encampment.

This was after they were under daily harassment from VC's mortars after building a helicopter airfield south of DaNang. We might of lost a some of our Nungs if we would of let them chase the VC any farther than they did the day after the probe of site 5 # because the marines lost about a dozen troops, but they killed a sizable number, but since the VC collect their casualties, they didn't have a count. With the exception of a few new prisoners, the VCs from Marble Mountains disappeared into the countryside.

This gave me some afterthoughts because as Don Raymond and I were training our Four Frogs for the Limpet attack on the Swatow Gunboats in 1962, we were within a few miles of Marble Mountains. In those days we were the only ones training on this whole beach (My Kye), and they must have known of our existence.

The SEALs expanded My Kye into five sites and a headquarters compound with the transfer to SOGMACV from SOGCIA (Combined Studies) in 1963. It was probably the same VCs that attacked the Special Forces camp at Hoa Com and killed our drinking buddies Spec Gabriel, Sgt Marchand, and captured Sgts Quinn, and Groom that they released on May 1st, 1962 as a propaganda move while negotiating for the release from prison of high priced VC officials. Remember in 1962 the war was still in the shouting and clandestine stages.

Note; After the NAD sites were abandoned in 1968, the Headquarters area became "China Beach", a recreational area for US service personnel. (This was made into a TV series for stateside showing)On my return to Coronado in 1964, and after the death of my Mother, I was engaged with the training of new transplants to SEAL One from the UDTs to ready them for deployment to Vietnam. SEAL Team One was expanding its number of personnel.

We had to wait while new replacements graduated from UDT replacement training and they were then simulated into the UDTs. We got the more experienced Frogs because to become a SEAL required far more experience to qualify than the replacement course did for the UDTs. By 1964-65 all SEALs were Parachute qualified, proficient in small arms, trained in small unit tactics ashore, Submarine escape trunk training, and knowledge of counter-insurgency warfare. In the beginning of the SEAL teams, all personnel were required to have two years of service in UDT. Due to the changing times that requirement started to SEAL detachments were now operating in the lower Mekong Delta, the Run Sat' Special Zone, and they continued with the Biet'Hai. The Run Sat' and Mekong Delta ops were without Vietnamese Forces. Some ops were made with the Riverine Boat Units, plus we had our own boats. Others were done largely from Helo insertions and extractions.

(The Sea Wolves) Operating with the Viets was compromised too often by intelligence leaks, so the SEALs stayed away from operating with any more than a single Viet interpreter. From a large number of successful ambushes and sweeps in the Rung'Sat and Mekong Delta, SEALs had built a reputation with the VC as warriors they should stay away from. Later when they started the PRUs of the Phoenix Program they would get the biggest, meanest Nung and put him in charge of security. That usually took care of any VCs that had infiltrated the unit. In 1965 I was given an operation to rescue two Nationalist Chinese Air Force Pilots that were on Hainan Mainland China (An Island in the Tonkin Gulf) this would be done from a US Navy Submarine, and it will be my next memoir.

Chief Petty Officer

Robert Sullivan

Naval Advisory Detachment

MACV SOG'S Naval Division

COMMENTARY AND ANALYSIS
CHAPTER EIGHT
MARITIME STUDIES BRANCH

MACVSOG - Command History Annexes A,N & M (1964-1966): First Secrets of the Vietnam War by Charles F. Reske

One of the most productive branches in the **SOG** organization was MACSOG-31, the Maritime Studies Branch. Possessed of an action arm known as the Maritime Studies Group (MACSOG-37), which operated under the cover name **Naval Advisory Detachment**, it had an excellent operational record from inception in 1964 to disestablishment in 1972.

The majority of naval operations against North Vietnam in 1964 were DeSoto patrols, which consisted of destroyers and aircraft operating in the Tonkin Gulf disassociated from all OPLAN 34A MAROPS .

In the event of a hostile attack, the patrol ships and aircraft were directed to fire upon the hostile attacker to insure destruction. Ships were to pursue the enemy to the recognized three-mile territorial limit, while aircraft were authorized hot pursuit inside territorial waters against surface vessels and into hostile airspace, (which included NVN, Hainan Island, and Mainland China) against attacking aircraft when necessary to achieve the destruction of identified attacking forces.

Originally, MAROPS had been designed to inflict psychological damage on the North Vietnamese by demonstrating the NAD/CSS ability to strike targets well above the 17th parallel. Destructive results and military utility were considered secondary, though U.S. aircraft were later added to the equation for cover operations above the 19th parallel.

Early OPLAN 34A operations were so successful that at one point the U.S. government considered going public with a handful of tangible victories to bolster the South Vietnamese and drum up popular American support for the growing war effort.

Typical 1964-1972 MAROPS---fine tuning, as such, of more conventional naval activities---consisted of shore bombardment utilizing Russian-made 122mm rockets mounted aboard PTF's (the so-called Nasty Class boats), junk captures, the kidnapping and disruption of the Viet Cong Infrastructure (VCI) in coordination with Provincial Reconnaissance Units below the 17th parallel, and Sea Commando Team demolition sorties against coastal radar, highways, and bridges. While SOG 31/37 possessed the capability for inland operations, most of their in shore coastal operations were of the shallow penetration variety,

Among the broad categories addressed in MACSOG-31 spot reports were such items as North Vietnamese paramilitary activities, air defense, conscription, coastal sea transportation, population controls, the identification of dissident groups, effects of the war on the NVN economy, and the governmental and popular reaction to friendly psywar activities.

SOG's concern over paramilitary activities extended beyond NVN support for the Viet Cong. One of the earliest issues addressed by the Maritime Studies Branch concerned the NVN effort to recruit and train Meo tribesmen. Since South Vietnam's relations with its own Montagnards lay somewhere between indifference and genocide, any attempt by NVN to win over a people born and bred to environmental hardship had to be viewed as a viable threat. **SOG's** experience with the capabilities of South Vietnam's tribal peoples convinced them that this was a legitimate consideration

In the area of psychological warfare, **SOG's** efforts revolved around gift kits, pre-set radios, and actions against North Vietnam's fishing industry. Despite great effort, the psywar operations garnered few positive results and constituted one of the least successful aspects of the covert maritime war.

Maritime Studies Branch, MACSOG-31, continued to exercise staff supervision and coordination for MACSOG covert maritime operations (MAROPS). MAROPS were conducted by the Martime Studies Group, MACSOG-37, under the cover name of Naval Advisory Detachment (NAD), Da Dang, in conjunction with the Coastal Security Service (CSS) of the Vietnamese Strategic Technical Directorate (SPD).

In Jan 71, under the direction of CINCPAC, Maritime Studies Branch developed five operation plans to support covert maritime operations against North Vietnam.

- 1. MACSOG OPLAN 5-70 (CLAY DRAGON): Utilized PTFs to transport Sea Commando Teams (SCTs) to designated targets along the North Vietnamese coast. The SCTs were to conduct amphibious raids against transshipment points to destroy/disrupt normal logistic flow.2. MACSOG OPLAN 2-'71 (BOSTON ANTIQUE): Utilized PTF's to intercept and destroy infiltration trawlers that had been designated a threat by CINPAC.
- 3. MACSOG OPLAN 3-71 (HAI CANG TUDO-2): Utilized PTF's to conduct shore bombardment of designated transshipment areas along the coast of North Vietnam.
- 4. MACSOG OPLAN 4-71 (GLYNN REEF): Utilized PTF's to destroy/disrupt the North Vietnamese fishing industry along the coast of North Vietnam.
- 5. MACSOG OPLAN 5-71 (HAI CANG TUDO-1): Utilized PTPs for interdiction of North Vietnamese coastal shipping along the coast of North Vietnam.

(TS) In mid-Feb 71, MACSOG-31 submitted to NAD a concept for mounting communist-made 122mm rockets on the PTFs. NAD developed the idea and installed the launchers by 1 Mar 71. Two salvos of four rounds could be fired in 15 minutes at a standoff range of 11,000 meters. The addition of the launchers significantly increased the PTP coastal bombardment potential. MACSOG OPLAN 3-1 was modified to include the new capability.

(TS) During Dec 71, JCS authorized the execution of MACSOG 3-71. Two missions were launched from Da Nang:

- 1. During the night of 26-27 Dec, four PTFs were ordered to conduct a 122mm rocket attack on QUANG KHE. The mission was aborted north of the 17th parallel due to extremely heavy sea conditions.2. During the night of 27-28 Dec, three PTFs were ordered to conduct a 122mm rocket attack on QUANG KHE and DONG HOI. While approaching the target the command PTF suffered an engineering casualty and had to abort. The other two PTFs attempted to close the target but were unable to do so due to the presence of enemy craft in the firing area.

SEA COMMANDO TRAINING

SCT training was exercised through DODGE MARK operations. These were supplemented by classes in ambush tactics, small arms firing, map and compass reading, rubber boat operations, and physical fitness. A training class in Oct-Nov 71 prepared 15 new Sea Commandos for integration into the unit and brought the total number of SCTs to five.   Editors note: *The above photo shows Sea Commandos and U.S Navy Seals after a mission.*

Looking to the south we see the harbor entrance control post at the very bottom of the photograph, in the middle is the observatory island where the Naval Advisory Group is located. In the foreground we see Tien Sha ramp and just south of that is the APL 30 where 600 men of the Naval Support Activity are berthed, 6 January 1966.

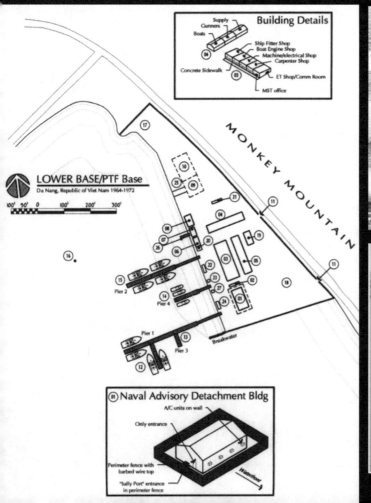

Building Details

Supply
Gunners
Boats
Ship Fitter Shop
Boat Engine Shop
Machine/electrical Shop
Carpenter Shop
Concrete Sidewalk
ET Shop/Comm Room
MST office

LOWER BASE/PTF Base
Da Nang, Republic of Viet Nam 1964-1972

100' 50' 0 100' 200' 300'

MONKEY MOUNTAIN

Pier 2
Pier 4
Pier 1
Pier 3
Breakwater

Naval Advisory Detachment Bldg

A/C units on wall
Only entrance
Perimeter fence with barbed wire top
"Sally Port" entrance in perimeter fence
Waterfront

Nasty boats at DaNang .

The Maritime star (NAD) would soon be eclipsed by SOG's ground operations in Laos, Cambodia, the DMZ, North Vietnam, and South Vietnam. But in 1964-6~ the Maritime Operations Section was riding high.

Charles F. Reske

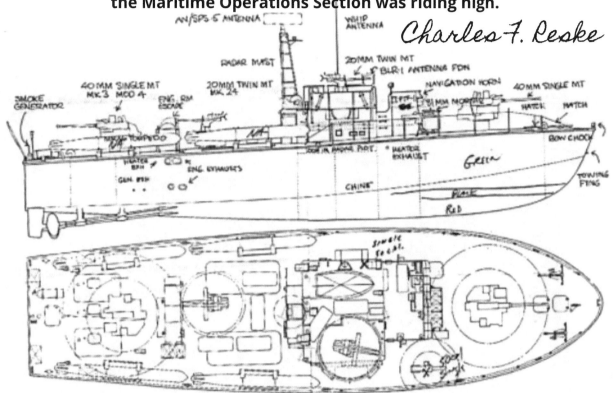

Nasty-class patrol boat

MACV SOG team near Danang 1971. The 2 Americans pictured are SEAL Team Echo, Bill Williams OIC, and the other is unknown. Originally the Naval Advisory Detachment had 1 American advisor and the rest were Vietnamese/Cambodian or former NVA. It was later changed to 2 SEALs, as pictured, or 2 Force Recon Marines per team per Gunny Norman Jennings advice. In the back ground are two nasty class PTF boats.

U.S. Navy Seals and their counterparts on a Nasty boat.

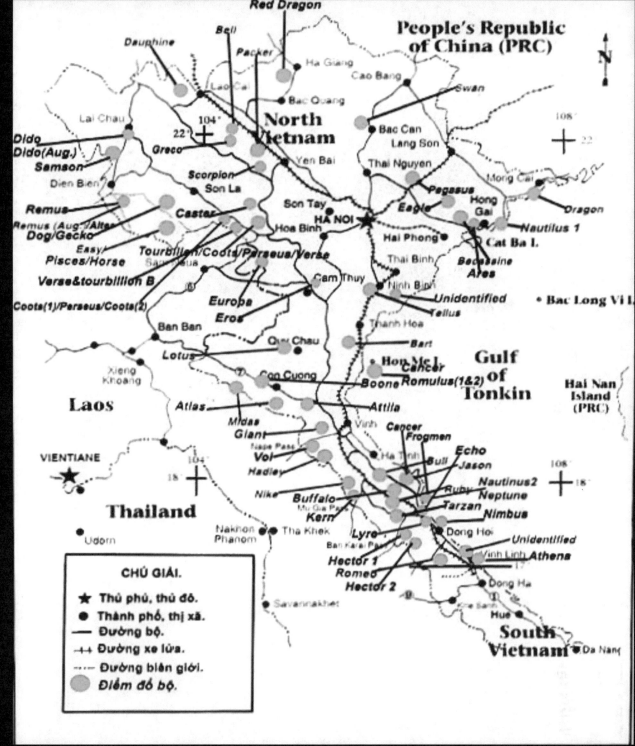

The map shows where thousands of insertions of ARVN MACV-SOG special operations teams had taken place in North Vietnam.